S0-CJD-674

THE MODERN COMMUNITY SCHOOL

CONTRIBUTING CHAIRMEN

PART I

SAMUEL EVERETT, *Professor of Education, The City College of New York*

PART II

KATE WOFFORD, *Head, Department of Education, The University of Florida*

PART III

RALPH SPENCE, *Executive Officer, Advanced School of Education, Teachers College, Columbia University*

OTHER AUTHORS

HARRY BARD, *Community Study Coordinator, Baltimore Public Schools*

LEONARD COVELLO, *Principal, Benjamin Franklin High School, New York City*

MARGUERITE J. FISHER, *Maxwell Graduate School of Citizenship and Public Affairs, Syracuse University*

LEWIS E. HARRIS, *Associate Director, Cooperative Program in Educational Administration in Ohio, Ohio State University*

DOROTHY G. HOLMES, *Supervisor of Rural Schools, Leon County, Florida*

MARGARET KOOPMAN JOY, *formerly Professor of Social Science, Central Michigan College of Education*

C. C. LOEW, *Superintendent of Schools, Urbana, Illinois*

DORIS MACGREGOR, *Elementary School Teacher, Springfield, Missouri, Public Schools*

MORRIS R. MITCHELL, *President, Putney Graduate School of Teacher Education, Vermont*

E. J. NIEDERFRANK, *Extension Rural Sociologist, United States Department of Agriculture*

SAMUEL POLATNIK, *Teacher, Benjamin Franklin High School, New York City*

MERLE R. SUMPTION, *Executive Officer for Field Service, University of Illinois*

JOAN B. WHITE, *Instructional Supervisor, Emanuel County Schools, Georgia*

SADIE K. ZION, *Elementary School Teacher, Philadelphia Public Schools*

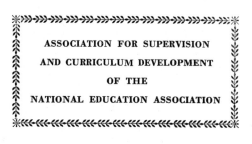

ASSOCIATION FOR SUPERVISION
AND CURRICULUM DEVELOPMENT
OF THE
NATIONAL EDUCATION ASSOCIATION

The Modern Community School

Association for Supervision and Curriculum Development. Committee on the Community School.

EDITED BY

EDWARD G. OLSEN

Education Director, Chicago Region
National Conference of Christians and Jews

LB
7
A873

APPLETON-CENTURY-CROFTS, Inc.

NEW YORK

83191

Copyright, 1953, by

APPLETON-CENTURY-CROFTS, INC.

*All rights reserved. This book, or parts
thereof, must not be reproduced in any
form without permission of the publishers.*

573–1

Library of Congress Card Number: 53-8986

PRINTED IN THE UNITED STATES OF AMERICA

Why This Book?

$\mathbf{M}$ILESTONES MARK OUR PATH of progress from the traditional, book-centered school of yesterday to the emerging, life-centered school of tomorrow. One such milestone is dated 1938—the year *The Community School* by Samuel Everett and his Committee on the Community School was published.[1] That volume, first to deal with the community school as such, emphasized the significance of the community approach in education, described in some detail the programs and principles of nine community schools, and analyzed their operations in terms of basic issues which seemed to distinguish the community concept from the conventional view. *The Community School* was a true pioneer; it blazed a trail for needed leadership; it interrelated school-and-community thinking and practice at its then best.

In these brief fifteen years since then (but what a deal of social change!) the community approach in education has won wide acclaim. The community school concept has been both expanded and refined; community education programs are everywhere developing. Recognizing this growth, the Executive Committee of ASCD felt that a fresh treatment of the community school field is now needed, and

[1] This was a committee of the old Society for Curriculum Study which was later merged with the National Education Association's Department of Supervision to become the Association for Supervision and Curriculum Development.

v

that such an analysis might prove valuable as further stimulus and guide. Accordingly, the present volume was authorized with the request that it give attention to "an enlarged concept of education which involves total community planning and use of resources." Accepting that broad directive, this new Committee on the Community School now presents its report which, it trusts, reflects the widening concept, describes some current best practice, indicates certain tested procedures, and suggests a basic value-frame of reference that is educationally sound and thoroughly democratic.

We have designed this book for lay leaders—for members of boards of education, parent-teacher associations, citizens committees, community councils—as well as for students of education, teachers, curriculum workers and school supervisors and administrators. We emphasize *direction, process* and *procedure* even as we present many case-studies, both real and fictional. We hope our thinking may serve as partial guide and renewed stimulus to further cooperative effort by American schools at all levels and their supporting communities which are always regional and national as well as local in scope.

How Was It Written?

Many people shared their experience and pooled their efforts to produce this book. Between 1948 and 1951 various members of the Committee met with the chairman in extended planning and criticism sessions at the successive ASCD conventions in Cincinnati, New York, Denver, and Detroit. In these many discussions major directions were decided, outlines developed and refined, group and individual responsibilities determined, basic philosophy examined and re-examined, better perspective always sought. Each year "open" committee meetings were held and were well attended; from these came scores of fine suggestions, many of which are incorporated in this report. After first-draft manuscripts were prepared they were duplicated and sent to Committee members, for their critical comments and suggestions. The final manuscript was read by the three section chairmen.

Part I was developed under the leadership of Samuel Everett, Chapter One's "projected accounts" were done by four writers: "The Visby School" by Morris Mitchell, "Timber Lake" by Margaret Koopman Joy, and "Metropolita, U.S.A." by Leonard Covello and Samuel Polatnik. Some implications of this community approach in education were then pointed up by Samuel Everett in Chapter 2, this serving as both summary and forecast.

Part II was drafted by Kate Wofford, utilizing much actual case-study material sent in by scores of teachers and others at Committee request. Cases which could be used are credited in the text; all others were deeply appreciated also. To provide even better representation among project types, kinds of communities, school levels and geographic locations, several case-accounts drawn from recent literature were later added by the editor.

In writing Part III, Ralph Spence utilized some materials and many suggestions offered by S. M. Corey, Gordon Mackenzie, Margaret Wasson and Kate Wofford. Harold Clark, Harry Bard and Lloyd Allen Cook aided in getting a more definitive statement.

The bibliography of films and other reference materials was provided by the editor, who also is responsible for the final organization of the volume. From the first inception of the whole project—and through eleven successive committee sessions over a four-year period—Prudence Bostwick most loyally helped to develop and refine the group thinking which finally produced this volume.

Committee, writers, critics, editor—all have labored together to present this second report on the community school by a committee of the ASCD. We offer it thoughtfully, trusting it may provoke continuing professional and lay interest, stimulate more bold activity toward better schools, and indicate desirable directions for more effective school-community cooperation in this troubled second half of our challenging twentieth century.

EDWARD G. OLSEN, Chairman
Committee on the Community School

CONTENTS

COMMITTEE ON THE COMMUNITY SCHOOL

WALTER K. BEGGS
University of Nebraska

GORDON BLACKWELL
University of North Carolina

PRUDENCE BOSTWICK
Denver Public Schools

HAROLD F. CLARK
*Teachers College
Columbia University*

LOIS M. CLARK
National Education Association

LLOYD ALLEN COOK
Wayne University

S. M. COREY
*Teachers College
Columbia University*

LEONARD COVELLO
*Benjamin Franklin High School
New York City*

C. LESLIE CUSHMAN
*Philadelphia
Public Schools*

SAMUEL EVERETT
*College of the City
of New York*

MARGARET KOOPMAN JOY
*formerly
Central Michigan College of
Education*

N. SEARLE LIGHT
*Connecticut State
Department of Education*

GORDON N. MACKENZIE
*Teachers College
Columbia University*

HOWARD Y. MCCLUSKY
University of Michigan

PAUL J. MISNER
*Glencoe, Illinois
Public Schools*

MORRIS R. MITCHELL
*Putney Graduate School
of Teacher Education*

EDWARD G. OLSEN
(Chairman)
*National Conference of
Christians and Jews*

CLARA M. OLSON
University of Florida

LEROY PETERSON
University of Wisconsin

SAMUEL POLATNIK
*Benjamin Franklin High School
New York City*

GLADYS POTTER
*Long Beach, California
Public Schools*

MAURICE F. SEAY
University of Chicago

WARREN SEYFERT
University of Chicago

RALPH B. SPENCE
*Teachers College
Columbia University*

WILLIAM VAN TIL
*George Peabody College for
Teachers*

MARGARET WASSON
*Highland Park Public Schools
Dallas*

KATE V. WOFFORD
University of Florida

xi

THE MODERN COMMUNITY SCHOOL

WARNING!

There are no blueprints in this book. This is not a guaranteed guide to the community school in ten easy lessons. The surest way to defeat any developing community education program is to take such reports as those presented here as magic formulas to be followed in step-by-step fashion. Because every community differs from all others in background, needs, resources and leadership, every community must design its own program in its own way. In this very fact lies the basic challenge and the finest promise of the community school approach to modern education.

PART

I

The Schools
We Need

*Part I presents three imaginative portrayals of com-
munity education in the 1960's, followed by a high-
lighting and evaluation which becomes in itself a basic
orientation to community school development. These
descriptions are framed, in turn, in a rural setting, a
small town, and a large city. Each statement is the
product of a professional imagination released from
the limitations of any single existing program, but
solidly grounded in the wide experience and insight
of its author.*

*These case-descriptions are bold sketches of what
American community education might become. They
are designed to stimulate thinking, to provoke comment, and to suggest desirable directions for school
program development. None is to be considered in
any sense a specific pattern to be accepted or followed
as such. All are individual's dreams, not educators'
blueprints.*

1

Schools of Tomorrow

THE VISBY SCHOOL
IS ITS COMMUNITY

THE RURAL SCHOOL OF TO-
morrow, fortunately, exists today. To see it one must travel
far. Its elements are scattered. They are to be found by
seeking out those exceptionally farsighted, courageous yet
judicious teachers who know the meaning of our times and
are allowed reasonable latitude by wise administrators
because constant readjustment in the educational process
is fundamental to sound instruction in our so-rapidly-
changing world. To save the time and cost of wide travel,
and to make more vivid the rural school of tomorrow, let
us assemble the fragments, now so widely scattered, at the
imaginary village of Visby in the southern part of a for-
ward-looking state.

Visby is a village of 750 people. It is a community of
three times this number, for the village is merely the
nucleus of the whole. There is not the dichotomy of town
and country. The bank does not own more and more of
the outlying land through foreclosures. Insurance com-
panies own none of it. The residential section is not confined to those who have moved to town to enjoy old age in
idleness. One does not there see farmers entering stores
whose books of profits and loss and charge accounts are
secret, and in which they humbly sell their products for a
low, set fee only to watch them resold immediately at ab-

3

surdly advanced prices. Nor does one see in Visby the
purchasing on credit at exorbitant rates, or perhaps worse,
the disappointment of the farmer who can neither buy for
cash nor secure credit. One sees no land exploited, nor
persons either. He finds rather a community relationship
of human harmony based on harmony between man and
nature.

There are eighteen commercial enterprises in Visby:
feed mill; general store, including departments of grocer-
ies, meats, produce, drugs, hardware, dry goods; telephone
central; fire department; moving-picture theater; creamery, with equipment for making butter, cheese, ice cream,
and powdered milk; a food storage plant with departments
of dehydration, canning, quick freezing and cold storage;
credit union; funeral parlor; livestock sales ring; livestock
breeders' association with facilities for artificial insemination; coal yard; lumber yard; a factory for educational
toys; restaurant; filling station and garage; shoe repair
shop; health clinic and hospital. Many of these enterprises
are co-operative, being owned and operated through open
and almost universal membership. The employees of these
firms and retired persons and their families compose the
residential area.

Visby reverses the usual procedure in being a town owned
by the surrounding farmers rather than one reaching out,
in octopus fashion, to own the outlying community. Ex-
hausted farmers and restless youth do not move to town to
build or buy on a loan a socially unneeded gas station, an
additional small store. The gas station and garage at Visby
is, like the other commercial institutions, a place of pride
and service to all—modern in design, ample in space, well
equipped, staffed with well-trained personnel. This station
is part of a regional organization having its own refinery
and also an interest in oil wells and still other refineries

owned by the central national co-operative association. The personnel are regularly students in the regional and national co-operative schools.

Architecturally, Visby is a planned village, for its co-operative philosophy reveals itself in every detail of physical and social existence. Too often our present-day towns reflect their lack of co-operation in striving for attention through the exhibitionism of inharmonious design in buildings, extreme height, unsightly display, and garish outdoor signs. In Visby signs serve only the function of guidance. The buildings are designed for use and fit severally into an over-all picture, blending with one another and into the landscape.

Education Goes to the People

The school is in one sense highly centralized; in another, highly decentralized. On the one hand there is a firm conception of an educational institution: an intense *esprit de corps* among the professional teaching staff, efficient administrative setup, adequate fiscal support and controls, ample instructional equipment, and records of individual activity and measurement of growth. But on the other hand, there is decentralization in the sense that education goes out to the people in their homes, finds them at work and play, and helps them in the thousand problems of life.

Specifically, there is no one monumental, factory-like building called the school. The campus is the community, which merges with other communities and regions into the nation and thus blends into world society. Not one building, but every building in Visby is considered an educational resource. The design of every building, its construction, care, and use, are all a part of the educational concern of the school. The whole structure of the community—its

total design as well as the development of all its details—
is a constant, if often unconscious, concern of nearly all
the citizens.

The community's layout and expansion result from the
will of the group based on decisions attained in joint consideration. Community beautification is a case in point.
Landscaping, which allows due latitude for individual preference in private homes—the growing of shrubbery, and the
propagation of trees—has largely come to be the responsibility of the school. The community nursery run by the
school comprises nine acres, a propagating house and a
greenhouse, constructed by the secondary students. The
nursery grows a great variety of ornamentals suited to the
local climate. The propagation of delicate ornamentals is
done by advanced students, who are also responsible for
budding, grafting and hybridizing. The more hardy plants
are cared for by the younger children. The only charge
made for plants is that minimum required to make the department of community beautification self-supporting. The
plants are used in the park, public square, around all public buildings, town residences and are used by country
homes as well.

If there is one central building of the school plant, it is
the library, or more properly, the "materials bureau." Here
one finds no vast collection of ancient books and textbooks.
Instead, there is a functional collection of the most modern
publications in each field of interest. Older books are obtained when needed from the state library. The bureau
circulates its films, charts, slides, pictures, models, recordings and transcriptions (including the best in music), language courses, and lectures to the public. There are scientific exhibits. Special rooms within the library are set aside
for the use of individuals and groups at study. These informal rooms, of varying size and types of furniture and

equipment, replace the older standardized school class-rooms. Consumer research and other scientific laboratories are also found, and are used by all age groups including adults. There is no one building with sufficient rooms for all of the children and youth of Visby to sit down simul-taneously at desks and pretend to an interest in dull texts. Here are no "grades," no "classes," but there are many groups brought together by common personal and social interests and their related problems. Sometimes these groups include wide differences in chronological age.

The recreation hall is in the center of the community park which comprises two square miles bordered by a river and lake. Landscaping has added to the beauty of the natural setting. There are out-of-door play facilities: canoe-ing, sailing, swimming, fishing, skiing, volleyball, tennis, golf, archery, basketball, baseball. It is a park for festivi-ties. Here the community gathers for singing each Sunday of open weather and on other occasions. There is an out-door theater. Frequently music is provided for folk dancing. Here is evident the colorful joyfulness of young and old in rhythmic play. In the hall there are comfortable chairs. Simple refreshments are available.

For the encouragement of hobbies, one building on the park grounds has been designed with separate, supervised rooms especially equipped for those interested in photog-raphy, radio, model airplane building, auto mechanics, chemistry, music, painting and so forth.

The park merges with the community-owned forest of 7,000 acres. In its center is a small sawmill, a steam kiln for drying lumber, storage sheds, a planer and a well-equipped shop where citizens may be assisted in the design-ing and making of furniture, toys, or even additions to their homes.

The forest is the joint responsibility of the secondary

and junior college groups. Since the forest comprises the drainage area for the village water supply, the utmost care in sanitation is essential. Once a frequently burned-over, scrubby area, the present community forest is one of the state's finest examples of a climatic growth. The deep mulch of fallen needles absorbs the rain virtually without runoff. Soil rich in humus is developing. Diseased trees are practically absent as are those infested with parasites. Crooked trees are cut into firewood or sold to paper mills. Between the forest and the park is an arboretum, a horticultural laboratory in itself. It contains more than one thousand varieties of shrubs and trees, each labelled with its common and scientific name.

The teachers are, first of all, competent people, then citizens, then teachers. Generally they are married. Community members are proud that among them are several races and groups, including Negro, Indian, Hindu and Japanese, for Visby believes that we cannot be one world until the principles of tolerance underlying communities such as theirs are universally adopted.

The Home Is the Center

To integrate their efforts, teachers hold meetings, make careful reports, and camp together on the lake island for several weeks each summer. But instruction is mainly in the home, whether by teachers, playmates, or parents. There are special teachers of art, music, homemaking, agriculture and the like, and each has a car for going to all parts of the community, which is some six miles in radius. Thus is overcome the impoverishing influence of the so-called consolidated school which strengthens itself at the expense of intimate contact with its more remote constituency.

The teachers counsel with each family according to the

field of specialization. The literature teacher, for example, visits the homes to encourage withdrawal from the library of suitable books as they are needed. Suggestions are not standard ones drawn from some state-compiled reading list. They are based directly on an intimate knowledge of the home life and immediate concerns of the family members. The literature teacher's car is a "bookmobile" with a constantly fresh assortment of materials, timely as regards seasons and the world's events. Similarly the specialist in agriculture carries with him needed scientific equipment, as for soil analysis, and appropriate volumes. A farmer is starting with bees, for example, so he is offered the best materials on apiculture. Though the calls of the teachers are professional, they are eminently friendly. Much of the best teaching, and learning, is done about the dining table.

So close is the working of parents, teachers, and youth that it is often impossible to make such distinctions. The study groups are a form of adult education in which "teachers" are simply members. But since these meetings usually are in homes and among small groups of neighbors, the young people are naturally drawn into the meetings and discussions. The co-operative commercial enterprises provide employment, and the managers count the giving of instruction to such employees an important duty. In this sense these managers are also teachers.

Instruction is usually informal, but it is not haphazard. In organization it becomes increasingly logical just as the mind itself does. In this there is no coercion. Groups form to seek a systematic understanding in one field or another. They dissolve when that purpose is met.

Recognizing that science is the basic cause of the bewildering recent social changes, Visby has sought to develop the scientific habit of mind through study. But Visby also

realizes that science, with its servant, technology, has increased our means of production far beyond our ability to
distribute equitably. Consumer co-operation to that end,
on a democratic basis, has therefore become the heart of
the social studies program. Thus two basic and interdependent purposes are deliberately kept in perspective:
scientific method and ethical use. The science hall is
equipped for real experimentation. The greatest variety
of hunches and hypotheses are here subjected to scientific
tests. And the results find their way into action. Thus by
careful test, a local walnut was found to exceed in thinness
of shell all known varieties by a margin so significant that
a government agency sent a specialist to Visby to cross-
pollinate the local tree with many other superior kinds
of walnuts.

Youth participates in an exhaustive study of natural resources—in minerals, in flora and fauna, in sources of
energy. Daily experience is habitually analyzed for problems needing scientific inquiry. In a number of homes in
Visby are to be found science laboratories of superior
equipment and remarkable activity. Some of these are
maintained by secondary school students; some are operated jointly by companions; several are distinctly family
enterprises where mother, father, and several children find
delight in pooling their inventiveness in furthering experiments.

All this is in strong contrast to the so-called textbook
"experiments" in which the "pupil" follows routine directions to almost inevitable conclusions. One sees the results
of such an approach to science in the alertness of the citizens in meeting the problems of home, farm, village. The
quality of living is lifted in myriad little ways. For instance, the younger citizens check on the number of bac-
teria per cubic centimeter in the community's sources of

milk. The community *knows*, because of their supervision, that all the cows are free from Bang's disease, tuberculosis and mastitis; that all cows stand on clean concrete floors, are milked in modern protected pails or by electric milkers; that the cows are fed clean, wholesome, nourishing food; that the butterfat content is approximately five per cent; that the cows are brushed before being milked, the udders washed and dried, and the milker's hands made sterile before the milking of each cow.

At the present time there are, over the nation, rural secondary schools in number which are reaching out into "real life situations" by installing and operating equipment such as canneries, storage houses, freezer locker plants, dehydrating plants, barber shops, beauty shops, printing shops, gardens, even farms. But these miss the challenge of our times unless they go beyond the problem of increasing productive capacity and solve the inescapable problem of social distribution.

Education for Civic Advance

Science, social distribution, wise resource-use—these are basic curricular elements at all grade levels at Visby, where citizens generally recognize the transition problems involved in moving from an economy of material scarcity into one of relative abundance within the democratic framework of society. Children, youth and adults in Visby study what has been going on in every land—in India, England, Union of South Africa, Sweden, Canada, Germany, Russia —in all countries, everywhere. Political leaders are to them not persons to be liked or disliked but symbols of social change, upheaval, in a time of unprecedented readjustment. The calm question is always "what is right?" not "who is right?"

Practice in democratic planning is gained through a special community planning council. A large room in the library where meetings can be held houses literature, charts, maps, and models. In architectural models one may see Visby as it was in each decade of its existence and in tentative projection for the future. No building is approved for construction until a scale model has been made and placed in its exact setting on the miniature landscape.

Students of photography annually make pictures of each structure of the community—that is, of the one hundred and thirty-six square miles of the community, not merely of the village itself. These are attached in proper relative position on roll maps which are as large as one wall of the planning room. On this map are laid out the streets, roads, forests, park, river. The dramatic development of Visby reveals itself as one studies the sequence of these student-made maps. Part of the conscious urge of the community toward a higher quality of living may be traceable to these studies.

Beyond individual and community planning there is frequent study of regional plans such as the TVA; the MVA; the AVA, the Columbia River Basin, and regional planning in other parts of the world as in Palestine and areas of India.

In the laying of plans, it is customary for trained counselors to point out to individuals and groups certain types of activities that have proved fruitful for growth. One of these is travel, another work—for farm-reared youth, in a factory; for village youth, on a farm. Field trips for a day or a week are arranged. On the secondary level the youth hostel movement is participated in. Junior college students and adults are encouraged to travel by "Youth Argosy" to Europe or even around the world. Hitchhiking is strongly discouraged, but hiking is characteristic of the community's interest in nature and in the larger world. Several groups of youth and adults have hiked the Appalachian Trail from Georgia to the northern extremity of Maine. Travel to foreign countries is regarded as practically essential to individual development and to community growth. Many of the secondary school students visit various parts of the world and all bring back to the community forum the benefits of their travel-study.

Travel, it should be noted, is not of the "excursion" or "sightseeing" type. Individuals and groups go out with plans made in advance to study a particular aspect of an area. Nearness to the Mesabe Iron range may prompt an interest, for example, in Kiruna, and the Swedish steel industry at Sandviken. A party is formed to visit these places. By the use of language records and language texts and with the aid of native-born Swedes, the party sufficiently masters the language to feel almost immediately at home in that Scandinavian country. Their purpose and plan and general study have been made known to the officials at Kiruna and Sandviken through correspondence and through mutual friends, and a warm reception awaits them. The records and the process of mining and manufacture are made readily available so that a deeper insight is gained than could come to a traveler who had made less careful plans. In Visby—as in all community schools—social travel is social study.

Such study is made relatively inexpensive by tourist rates and youth hostels, by frequent self-propelled methods of transportation such as hiking, canoeing, bicycling, and through accumulated wisdom in the art of simple travel.

Beyond the Ruts

Visitors are coming increasingly to study Visby and its unique program. All leave with a deep respect for the culture that is revealed in the high standard of living, the peacefulness and beauty of the village and countryside, and the profound courtesy that one universally meets. Most, though, are confused by the school's innovations and by the absence of many of the attributes of "school" that they have unconsciously presumed to be indispensable. They do not find it easy to perceive that education and living are inevitably one; that sound education for today is intelligent and ethical individual and community living. There can be no sound education in an unsound community. There is no use talking about the improvement of rural instruction until teachers and citizens generally lift their eyes, as have those in Visby, beyond the ruts of the road and work actively toward democratic living in a world of peace based upon a universally shared economy of plenty.

TIMBER LAKE HAS
A COMMUNITY SCHOOL

Timber Lake with its 12,452 people was officially termed an "urban community" after the 1950 United States Government Census was compiled. But those who live there speak of "going to town" when they drive in sixteen miles from their farm to buy the children's fall school shoes, visit a neighbor who is in the Community Hospital, or see the 4-H exhibit at the Northern District Fair. Some folks who live in Timber Lake consider it a "city"—the mill-owning families of lumber days, the professional men, and the people who run small businesses which serve the town, the resorts, and the rural area for twenty-five miles around.

For 40 years Timber Lake was one of several important lumbering towns in its area. First the pine was cut, then the hardwood. The last of the logging camps, saw mills, and planing mills closed during the First World War. A few related industries continued to run—a veneer plant, a table factory, a chair factory, and a small foundry. These gradually declined and virtually disappeared during the early 1950's, giving way to branches of industries which are decentralizing and moving out from the large metropolitan areas. Meanwhile the industrious Scandinavian, Dutch, and "Yankee" woodsmen and homesteaders turned their entire attention to farming the most fertile land. Today they have the highest income from agriculture of any community in the northern cut-over area.

Other families who settled on the barren hills and sandy out-wash plains to the southeast, referred to locally as the "pine plains," eventually saw the futility of farming there and either moved to town or sought work in the rapidly growing tourist and resort industry. Hundreds of acres of this sub-marginal land was eventually taken over as part of a National Forest, and today is the paradise of fishermen, the hunting grounds of sportsmen, and the winter playground of old and young who enjoy skiing and tobogganing.

Timber Lake has always been proud of her schools. The high school, however, was originally designed to serve only the sons and daughters of the ministers, doctors, lawyers, lumbermen, and storekeepers of the town. The educational program operated on that basis until the post-war recession in the early 1920's revealed not only the economic insecurity of the community, but the inadequacy of the school system as well. The per cent of dropouts in the academic, college-preparatory high school rose, while demands for youngsters in the labor market fell. Boys and girls who succeeded in finding work soon discovered that they were in dead-end jobs. There was wide-spread idleness and discouragement, and relief rolls lengthened. Juvenile delinquency increased.

Then a change of leadership occurred in the State Department of Education. Something new was being advocated—the democratic "community" school. Timber Lake's old superintendent retired and the Board hired a new man.

Professional Leadership

What the new superintendent lacked in experience he made up in social insight and professional zeal. It was from him that the teachers, parents, and youngsters first heard of the community school. He contended that school and community are inseparable, that children and youth cannot be educated solely within the four walls of a school, that the school should help to acquaint the people with local, regional, national and world resources for education and community improvement, and should furnish direction and leadership for the fullest use of these resources.

Because of this challenge teachers and interested laymen began to realize that a school in a community such as Timber Lake is not serving its purpose unless it provides for the real educational needs of every child, youth and adult in the community. The improvement of the quality of human living, both personal and social, became accepted as the function of education in Timber Lake.

A more democratic pattern of school administration and in-service training then began to emerge. Natural leaders in school and community formed the Timber Lake Com-

munity Council. This council has for 12 years worked steadily to make Timber Lake a better community in which to
live and rear a family.

During the last 15 years school district reorganization
has brought all outlying rural districts into the Timber Lake
Community School District. The district now includes several neighborhood elementary schools, in walking distance
for many of the children, a central high school and a community college built at the south side of town on a 130-acre
tract of land. The schools now serve the community, and
the community is part of the "school."

Buildings, grounds, equipment, recreational facilities,
and the personnel of the schools are made available to any
group which is helping further the well-being of the people.
School groups, in co-operation with civic groups or public-
spirited persons, initiate and carry on community better-
ment projects under the competent direction of their teachers and volunteer community leaders.

Education is not limited to children and teen-agers. All
the citizens in town and country use the educational resources of the Community School in solving the problems
of day-by-day living and in enriching their personal lives.
They recognize the fact that some of their youth will stay
in Timber Lake. Others will find their satisfactions and
opportunities elsewhere. All should experience a wholesome childhood and youth, which will fit them for competent living in a free world.

Now they believe that the major purpose of education is
life-long participation of all persons in effective, democratic
social living, and that each individual should have equal
opportunity for the fullest possible development of his own
capacities. To achieve these ends they are working continuously toward a democratic way of life in home, school
and community.

Lay Participation

Administrators, teachers, boys and girls, and representative lay people now share in policy making, curriculum planning, and in establishing desirable standards of human relationships. A Policy-Forming Committee has been very active in setting up criteria for a co-operative school government, regulations for the use of school facilities by community groups, and is now developing policies and plans for working constructively with pressure groups.

Committees which are broadly representative of the school and the people operate as creative working groups. It is one of these committees which recently gained national recognition for its curriculum in home and family living, a program which has stood up under rigorous evaluation.

Another working group, in co-operation with the Timber Lake Community Council and the high school and community college classes in social relationships, has explored the economic resources, job opportunities, and labor supply of the community and the region. Their findings have served as a guide for education for economic competence. This program includes vocational guidance and exploration, on-the-job training, and numerous group projects in homemaking, agriculture, and conservation, consumer education, and the management of a marketing co-operative.

The work-experience program required of all older youth takes young people into varied responsible work situations during the second half of their high school program.

Timber Lake's Committee on Human Relations has recently been engaged in an ambitious project in group dynamics. It has attempted to define the role of administrators, teachers, parents, and students in school and community life. Its work has furnished a sound basis for planning basic school policies with people, and has been used in parent education and in-service teacher education.

The Role of the Teacher

To date, most of this committee's attention has been directed to the role of the teacher in a democratic community school. It is the consensus of the Committee on Human Relations that this role should be one of democratic leadership and should involve the following kinds of behavior:

1. The teacher in our school will set up a provocative environment for learning and extending desirable pupil experiences and will use stimulating books, magazines, visual and auditory aids, manipulative materials, scientific equipment, and community resources.

2. The classroom will serve as a social laboratory where pupils under the leadership and counsel of the teacher set up necessary controls for living together democratically and directing their own activities.

3. The teacher will help each pupil understand interpersonal and intergroup relationships, find a place in the group, and become a contributing member of the group enterprise.

4. The teacher will guide pupils in setting their goals and progressing toward them—choosing learning experiences, allocating responsibility for fact-finding, sharing these findings, thinking through problems, reaching conclusions, carrying out an action program, evaluating outcomes.

5. The teacher will make a continuous effort to discover each pupil's capacities, interests, tastes, and habits, recognize them as signs of growing power, and help reveal them to the student himself in order to guide him in his own development.

6. The teacher, on an equal footing with other educated adults, will participate in projects for the promotion of community welfare and will guide pupils in community and world service projects.

This definition of the teacher's role furnishes criteria by which teachers are selected because they are willing and able to work in a democratic community school. It is used in judging their competence during the probationary period and in making later professional promotions. Teachers, in working with boys and girls, turn to the Committee on Human Relations for help in improving human relationships in school and community.

Timber Lake chooses its teachers carefully and pays them well. Therefore it can keep them long enough so that they become accepted and contributing members of the community.

Laymen and school people together have worked out a Career Salary Schedule which facilitates retention of master teachers who have the salary and professional status of other well-educated men and women in the community. Timber Lake's teachers are among the community's home owners, hospital board members, Scout leaders, Councilmen, Rotarians, and supper club members. They are "of us," not the "strangers" that sociologists find them to be in a vast number of communities.

Migrant Council

The only minority group in Timber Lake is the Spanish-speaking migrants who live there from April until November. They thin, weed, and top beets and pick snap beans and cucumbers. These workers contribute much to the prosperity of the farmers, and on their arrival are welcomed by members of the Migrant Council. They are encouraged to send their children to school and, as family groups, to participate in civic life.

The schooling of these children is badly interrupted as they follow the crops. A summer school has therefore been developed to meet their special needs. There is a nursery for pre-school children whose mothers work. There is tutoring in skill subjects for retarded pupils, and an integrated elementary school program for different age groups. Every effort has been made to avoid segregation. Boys and girls from local "Anglo" families are encouraged to go to summer school and avail themselves of this opportunity to learn Spanish in a natural setting, share experiences with children of a different cultural background, participate in day-camp, and enjoy arts and crafts, music, dancing, and dramatic play-experiences too often disregarded in rural areas. Thus many migratory workers, motivated partly by others' appreciation of Spanish, seek to increase their own abilities in Spanish as well as English language self-expression.

Areas of Living

The school, in co-operation with the Community Council, helps the people of Timber Lake identify and analyze community problems. Both in school and out they work toward their solution. An integrated curriculum has been developed around the major social processes: making a living, utilizing natural resources, maintaining a home, sharing in citizenship, securing an education, maintaining health, worshiping, enjoying leisure time, and building good human relationships.

Illustrative of this curriculum is the program of health education. Preliminary to curriculum building, three studies were made. First, a study was done of the interest and problems of pupils at all age levels regarding health, sex, and emotional attitudes. Second, a study of nutrition was made by teachers as part of their in-service education program. With the help of the nutritionists in the State Depart-

83191

ment of Health, a careful survey was made of the nutritional patterns of school children. Third, the Health Committee of the Community Council made a survey of the health needs of the community. The findings of these three studies were used in planning a functional health curriculum which has reached both children and adults.

Among the projects which have grown out of this program are the building of a health center as part of the school plant, a well-baby clinic, classes for expectant parents, consultative services in nutrition for school and club groups, and establishment of a flourishing health cooperative.

Learning Resources

Students are given firsthand information concerning community life and problems through the use of resource visitors. People are proud of their Laboratory for Life Studies in the community college. In a comfortable reading room they have available local histories and documents, newspaper files, survey-analyses of the Timber Lake community, U. S. Census Reports, government bulletins covering a wide variety of subjects, a complete collection of significant community studies, and books on the community school. A directory of consultants who can be secured from community, state, and national agencies is there for teachers and community leaders to use.

The library long since developed into a comprehensive "learning resources center" which stocks and circulates films, slides, pictures, recordings, transcriptions, models and exhibits as well as books, both standard and on microfilm. "Textbooks" are no longer used as veritable scriptures, but numerous and varied volumes are in constant use. The center operates under the direction of a young person fully trained in modern curriculum needs and practices. Since the completion of the new television cable from Europe last year and through national coverage people of all ages can witness many televised events of world significance as they occur, both at home and abroad. The community college's recording laboratory photographs all noteworthy events directly from the large viewing-screen; thus the community is building up a visual history-in-the-making file for future use in the schools. In their Communication Studies young people and adults are taught to analyze propaganda and to evaluate and select good radio, television and motion picture programs. Money for all these developments could hardly be secured until the Citizens Committee for the Public Schools became strong in the community. Since then nearly all informed citizens have *demanded* that the schools receive sufficient finances to provide adequate education for their children.

Timber Lake Community School considers it a major responsibility to help interpret national and world issues to the local community. To this end the school brings in consultants from private foundations, national associations, and state and federal agencies. In co-operation with the State University and a national association on community organization, an annual Community Life Conference is held. For two days youth and adults practically live at school. They share potluck meals, play together, and with the help of local leadership and outside experts discuss problems related to consumer buying, recreation, religion, and the like.

The Community Forum runs weekly throughout the long winter. Crowds turn out to see socially-significant films and televised programs, and stay to discuss problems of a troubled world. Sometimes high school and community college classes with their teachers put on panels to point up

the discussion. Occasionally a nationally-known speaker
or a celebrated musician is engaged and, at a nominal
charge, the community auditorium is packed. Another contact with the world outside comes through group visits to
other communities which have outstanding educational programs. The citizens believe in the comparison and evaluation of social agencies, schools, and communities so that
Timber Lake citizens may develop wider perspectives upon
their own lives in relation to the community and larger
world.

Laboratory for Learning

Boys and girls find answers to many of their questions
not only in the laboratory but also by going into the community and interviewing, conducting surveys, taking study
trips, and participating in community group activities.
Now that young people vote at age 18, far greater emphasis is placed upon practical citizenship through local and
regional service projects as well as through firsthand observation of government agencies and student internship in
them. The students recognize the values of a purposeful
program of studies and therefore do their part in making
the community, the region, the nation and the world at large
a laboratory for effective learning.

Local as well as extended study tours became common-
place during the 1950's. The school now owns three buses
equipped with loud speakers and two medium-sized planes
so that effective field trips are standard procedure. Three
years ago the school joined the International High School
Travel Association. This year a large group from the senior
class is spending its first semester on a travel tour of eastern
Europe. To house youth groups which come to the community a dormitory addition to the gymnasium was built

last year. Many of these student travel groups come from abroad, now that UNESCO is exchanging each year some three and a quarter million older youth between Asia, Europe, and the Americas.

Teacher exchanges, also arranged by UNESCO, add much to the community's international understanding. Last year one of the fourth-grade teachers exchanged classrooms with a Scottish teacher, and a high school teacher exchanged positions with a teacher in Japan. The foreign language teachers are frequently natives of countries using those languages. A committee of teachers, pupils, parents, and club and church representatives plans carefully the use of services of both the teachers from abroad and the returned teachers, for furthering international understanding among the people.

These teacher and pupil exchanges began during the "cold war" period of the mid-century and have been expanding ever since. It was in 1949 that Timber Lake began its successful affiliation with the comparable community of Skios in Greece. The community is proud to have helped pioneer this notable movement. In 1949 only about two hundred American communities had actively affiliated with similar towns abroad, in contrast to more than nineteen thousand such affiliations today.

Timber Lake is just one of the thousands of small town communities in America. But to its people it is unique and is "home town." While making surveys and assessing the community's strengths and its shortcomings, "ordinary citizens" develop a strong emotional attachment to the homeplace. They feel sure that by capitalizing on their natural and human resources and working co-operatively through their community school for the common welfare, they can create a good community and a better world with people who exemplify the democratic way of life.

COMMUNITY EDUCATION
IN METROPOLITA

The vibrant tempo of life in Metropolita can clearly be observed at any monthly meeting of the Citizens Council. To such sessions come the heads of the city service agencies, and what is even more significant, the representatives of the thirty major communities which comprise Metropolita.

During the 1940's and 1950's increasing numbers of people realized that better city existence requires more than the efforts of elected officials. The growing complexity of living in a city boasting millions of residents, tremendous industrial and commercial activities, numerous cultural patterns, and a whole host of problems and needs finally brought Metropolita's Citizens Council into being in 1958. It resulted structurally from an elaborate survey of the major sociological groupings to be found in Metropolita.

Thirty such groupings, or local communities within the great city, were finally established. In each of these subdivisions Community Councils were set up. Each local grouping determined the specific size of its Council and Executive Committee which were responsible for securing community-wide participation, co-ordination, and action. All thirty send two representatives to the monthly meetings of the Metropolita Citizens Council.

Since the organization of Metropolita's Council and its related local community councils and committees, a smoothly-working relationship has developed between the metropolitan area Council and the various community councils. The area-wide committee has served to call local

attention to metropolitan-wide matters, has become a re-
pository for local "know-how," has made it easier for local
communities to utilize city facilities in the solution of local
problems, and has served to channel local leadership into
the city service.

The most vital agencies in the whole process, however,
consist of the local community councils and the secondary
schools around which they tend to center. Each community
has found the need for meeting places, trained consultants,
"leg men," and long-range training of all citizens in active
community participation. In each community, experience
has shown that the community secondary school can best
serve as the focus for the local program.

Fellow Citizens!

Several years after the institution of the Metropolita
organization, a heated session is under way at a meeting of
the Metropolita Citizens Council. All delegates from the
local community councils are present. Joe Roberts, the
enterprising principal of Midvale High, is on his feet. Let's
listen.

Fellow citizens [he begins], we've learned a few things about
finding the concerns of all our people and of translating those
concerns into action. We've made changes in our school services
and programs to bring both young people and older folks into
the stream of community and city events. We've helped bring
better housing to some of our communities. We've seen the development of school-and-community-sponsored local newspapers.
We've contributed to the growth of more and better recreation
areas. We've improved educational budgets, and we've helped
new migrant groups in our communities to make better adjust-
ments to life in Metropolita.

Yet the people in the Midvale community, whom I have the

honor to represent, feel that we really have not done all we can. Our residents, who are typical of the citizens of many other Metropolita communities, are 20,000 strong. We have representatives of many cultural groups though predominantly we are Italian, Puerto Rican, and Negro. We are crowded like so many of the rest of those in Metropolita into a rather congested area. We confront problems of sanitation, health, and real livability. Newcomers in the constant flow of migrants face the need for learning a new language, require assistance in the citizenship process, and have to learn group responsibility for community and democratic living which may have been alien to the land of their origin. Many residents face problems of intergroup relationships. We have talked about these things in many of our local communities for a long time.

Serious juvenile delinquency exists for us, and perhaps for many of your communities also, because of the many second-generation children. In many families composed of foreign-born parents and American-born children, traditions of family solidarity, obedience, respect for elders, and subservience to family needs and requirements clash with the so-called American ideal of "living one's own life."

Our people in Midvale feel that we ought to generate a tremendous community and city pride in a project which will contribute to better living for all; that will give us all a chance to work together on a metropolitan-wide scale. And—we have the project! What we're after is to create a bright and glowing city area by a "Colorful Living Campaign." We think we need to get rid of drabness and disorder in our surroundings. For confusion and ugliness we must substitute order and beauty. What we mean is this: if we could only tap the full resources of the people in our community, and the resources that could be made available to us from the city at large, we could make city streets sparkle, make buildings reflect local character, have home interiors mirror the rich heritage of our cultural diversity. We think that we haven't done enough to make people smile in the joy of zestful surroundings!

Midvale's suggestion is taken up with enthusiasm by the Metropolita Council. As soon as the meeting ends, the delegates return to their local community councils to consider in detail the potential of their own communities for "more colorful living." Joe Roberts loses no time in telling his fellow Midvalites how well their suggestion was received.

Fellow Students!

The Midvale Council soon agrees that in the task now to be undertaken—surveying the beautification needs in Midvale, publicizing results, eliciting community-wide exchange of ideas, developing local action—the initiative should be taken by Midvale High. Next steps are therefore referred to the existing school-community committee, composed of students, faculty, parents, and other local residents.

Under the leadership of Frank Rodriguez, student president of the school's General Organization, the school-community committee calls a general assembly of Midvale's 3,000 students. This is held in three sessions to make accommodations in the assembly hall easier.

Fellow students [Frank announces], we've been given a chance to put Midvale on the map in a big way. Every community in the city is tackling a colorful living program. I think our school can show the way.

Here's what we've got in mind. We Midvalers are going to be asked to interview all the folks on our home blocks to get any community beautification ideas our people may have. The publications office is preparing mimeographed questionnaires, and block maps on which to note anything we see requiring action. You'll hear more about all this during your "community-study" hour.

As the morning assembly breaks up, Bob Smith, Gail Prince and other students go to the publications office. There they find everything needed for the survey in readiness because some time ago Midvale High had found that effective community action requires a block-by-block coverage. Since then all students have been asked to fill out enrollment cards on a residence basis. These are grouped according to residence-block. A residence-block was defined as all residents on a block whose homes face each other, thus taking in both sides of the street. Where no students from a residence-block attended Midvale, volunteers were selected from surplus students living in other blocks.

The publications office is organized to meet many problems of community publicity and action. Because it serves a multilingual community, its staff of students and adult advisers prepares materials in several languages. Publications also share space with Midvale High's other avenues of publicity. The school's radio and television studio occupy the same wing of the building as the publications office so that all these groups can work together in getting out important messages to the community. This combined public-relations unit is also responsible for the operation of the school's two sound trucks, which are used when necessary to bring a message requiring personal contact for maximum effectiveness.

The Curriculum Is Flexible

As the students of Midvale High survey their community, data begin flowing back to the school. It thus becomes necessary to consider what further analysis and activity are now necessary. Since the curriculum of Midvale High is so flexible, it is possible to focus school-wide attention on the new campaign without serious interruption or disturbance of intramural school activities.

The curriculum at Midvale High is not only adapted to the seventh- through fourteenth-grade students; it provides also for all the adults (defined as persons 18 years of age and over) in the community. This curriculum and schedule (see pages 32-35) is subject to continuous evaluation and change. It operates on a five-day basis (the building being available on Saturdays and Sundays for special events such as festivals, shows, club meetings, recreation, games, from 8:00 A.M. to 12:00 P.M. or later, as the need determines). The school operates continuously throughout the year, although not all students attend at all times. Adequate provision is made for individual vacations, travel and work opportunities at any season, while school camping and supervised work experiences are characteristic curricular activities at all times.

The school day is organized in three major divisions. Most of the adolescents (seventh- through twelfth-grade students) are provided for in the 8:30 A.M. through 3:30 P.M. schedule. However, where necessary, provision is made for students to take their work in another part of the day. The schedule from 3:30-7:00 P.M. provides for the recreational needs of youth and the educational and recreational needs of adults. In this same period the thirteenth- and fourteenth-year Community and Technical Institutes are in active session. From 7:00 to 10:00 P.M., provision is made for other groups, the major emphasis being placed on meeting the leading interests of the adults. Similarly, adults may participate in school work at any time during the school day. This is very important, particularly in urban communities where many adults work evenings, or on night shift.

The curriculum for secondary students contains several interesting features. Every boy and girl meets a prescribed two-and-a-half-hour daily core and a one-hour community problems requirement. Two hours are allotted for elective specialization.

Each of these categories requires further clarification. The core is required of every student for six years. This provides for the basic skills, knowledges and understandings, through work on problems and projects of an ascending scale of difficulty. Selected by the students with the help of the core teacher, these problems allow for experience and drill in oral and written communication skills, reading techniques, social studies, applied mathematics and science, music, art, literature appreciation, and health education. Since the problems dealt with tend to center about aspects of community life, instruction is really functional. Reading, for example, is not thought of as something in and of itself, but rather as a means towards desired ends— leisure, research, knowledge, and understanding. Stress throughout is placed on student planning, execution, and evaluation. Individual differences are taken into account in the distribution of work to be done.

CURRICULUM OF THE MIDVALE YOUTH SCHOOL

DIVISION I. Seventh- through Twelfth-Year Program

I. Prescribed Core:

A. *General Education*

2½ hours daily
(8:30 A.M.–11 A.M.)

Sharing in citizenship
Using communication tools
Building human relations
Improving family living
Developing economic competence
Protecting life and health
Enjoying wholesome leisure
Satisfying spiritual needs
Appreciating beauty
Meeting vocational responsibilities

B. *Community Service*

1½ hours daily (11 A.M.–12:30 P.M.)	Service projects at community centers, welfare and educational agencies, on school-community committees, in community research, etc.

II. Elective Specialization: (2 hours daily—1:30 to 3:30 P.M.)

A. *Pre-professional Studies*

Advanced science	Foreign languages
Advanced mathematics	Classics of world literature
Advanced social science	Techniques of playwriting
Ethics and philosophy	Etc.

B. *Vocational Preparation*

Automotive shop	Business machines
Ceramics	Commercial law
Electronics	Civil service preparation
Horticulture	Office practice
Plastics	Salesmanship
Photography	Stenography
Machine shop	Etc.
Etc.	

C. *Community Service Training*

Group leadership	Using communication media
Community analysis techniques	Planning community action
Reducing intergroup tensions	Etc.

DIVISION II. Afternoon Program for Youths and Adults
(Groups meet from 2 to 2½ hours between 3:30 and 7 P.M.)

Day school makeup courses for those unable to take work
during day

> Community problems
> Getting along with people
> Language study for non-English speakers
> Child care
> Building a home
> Budget buying
> Reading for enjoyment
> Interior decoration
> Music appreciation
> Charm and personality
> Etc.

DIVISION III. Evening Program for Youths and Adults
                          18 and Over

(Groups meet from 2 to 3 hours between 7 and 10 P.M.)

Day school makeup courses for those unable to take work
during day.

   A. *Cultural*

> Great books
> Art appreciation
> Music appreciation
> Study of human behavior
> Painting and sketching
> Choral singing
> Sculpture
> Puppetry
> History of Western Civilization
> The Eastern World
> Language study
> Etc.

   B. *Vocational and Technical*
       Radio, television repair
       Electrical shop
       Furniture repair
       Machine shop
       Plumbing
       Woodworking shop
       Photography shop
       Plastics
       Etc.

   C. *Commercial*
       Typing
       Stenography
       Business machines
       Salesmanship
       Etc.

   D. *Community Improvement*
       Communication of ideas
       Leading a meeting
       Home planning
       Building maintenance
       Action techniques
       Etc.

   E. *Basic Tools*
       English for the non-English speaker
       Basic mathematics
       Etc.

Community Service Required

Every student is required to give 90 minutes a day, throughout his entire school career, to community problems. This responsibility takes many forms. It involves discussion of, and participation in, many phases of school and community life. It includes such activities as assistance in the co-ordinating councils' research bureaus; work on the school-community newspaper, radio and television programs; participation in community surveys, membership on the school-community committees already described, service at social service agencies, work for community agencies, meeting with advisers and counselors to plan community projects and individual development, assistance at the school nursery and participation in student self-government projects. Such activity, conducted under trained supervision, aims at developing, early in a student's life, a feeling of responsibility for community effort, experience in actual and regular participation in significant common activity, and a basic know-how which may serve him in good stead in adult life.

Scheduled just before lunch, these community-service experiences allow the participants to continue on into the socializing activities of the noon hour. This does not, however, limit community activity to one part of the day. Interested students are able to carry community problems into other aspects of the school program, notably the hours spent in the core curriculum.

Individualized Program

Provision is made for individual differences and interests in the elective specialization made available to every person. Each student devotes two hours a day to specialized training for vocational competence and civic service. Students thus explore different career areas and begin early specialization determined by their abilities and interests.

Such a program necessitates special procedures in recording and reporting promotion and graduation. Record-keeping is largely anecdotal and represents a cumulative record of experiences noted by teachers. Records include observations made by community people who have observed the students' activities, diagnostic and prognostic tests, health records, and samples of the work of the students. Periodic reports to parents are descriptive of achievement and include personality and development evaluations by teachers and counselors in the Guidance Department. The records also include an inventory of all social and community agencies which have had contact with the child and his family. In recent years all community agencies have found it helpful to maintain this centralized "family-inventory" record at the school.

Promotion and graduation are made on the basis of successful completion of a prescribed number of hours of core, community, and specialized activities. Every effort is made to assist students to find activities of potential success. While promotion from grade to grade takes into account the relationship of achievement to capacity, applications to college include certification by the principal and the Guidance Department as to the level of capacity and achievement. Colleges, community institutes, and other institutions of higher learning commonly recruit their students upon this basis.

Operation of the 3:30-7:00 P.M. and the 7:00-10:00 P.M. schedules is on a less formal basis. Here the basic principle is to furnish leadership, facilities, and supplies to any group of adults which wishes to learn anything of practical, recreational, or cultural value. Any group of 20 adults can petition the principal for such service, and he has the responsibility of meeting their request. While these groups meet from two to three hours once or twice a week, intensive courses, meeting five evenings a week, are provided for those desiring such special training.

Personnel Services

All students, young and old, enjoy the advantages of health services, student self-government and personal guidance. There are available an employment counseling bureau, social welfare aid, home instruction for incapacitated children, visiting nurses, psychiatric testing and counseling and other assistance. In all this activity, the school seeks to encourage such help through the fuller utilization of the services of existing community agencies before assuming direct responsibility itself.

All teachers contribute to the accumulation of data to be used as basis for guidance and are assisted by a special Guidance Department. This Department includes a school doctor, school psychiatrist, head counselor, vocational placement expert, and several social workers. The Department maintains a constant review of each student's cumulative record and furnishes guidance summaries to each student as needed. Evaluation is made of progress to date and suggestions offered for the future. Where no special problems exist, guidance recommendations are periodically discussed by the core teacher with the student and his parents. When special difficulties arise the Guidance Department meets as a group, with the individual student, to discuss his needs. Staff members are assigned similar responsibilities for adults who may have difficulties of one kind or another.

Such a curriculum makes it easy for John Stewart, a 16-year old in the eleventh year, Betty Klein, a 15-year old in the tenth year, and Mr. Ray Marchetti, a local florist, to participate in the community campaign for colorful living.

Sharing Enthusiasms

John's core group had been considering "Housing Needs in Our Community." They now intensify their efforts. They make maps of land use, investigate land values, and compile statistics on average incomes. John finds himself interviewing tenants and landlords on living facilities, apartment beautification, street appearance, and the like. With the help of the Midvale Community Advisory Council, the class is enabled to hear members of the City Planning Commission. They proceed to write letters to local political, civic, business, and religious leaders urging effective action. With the help of the art staff, they build models of the kind of community they would like to live in, and invite architects and planning engineers to appraise their efforts. Displays of student ceramics and shop work, which could be used in homes, are set up in the windows of many local stores.

Betty's group uncovers a special problem. A new immigrant group resides in the area her class has surveyed. Unaccustomed to American ways of sanitation, these people often pitch or "air-mail" garbage out of their windows. Betty and her classmates recognize that this is a ramified problem of community education. Bob Murphy suggests that what might be needed first is a greater effort to integrate these newcomers into the regular life of the community. Dina Tessitelli suggests that the class sponsor a community festival. Some youngsters write to the leaders of various cultural groups in the community, asking for support and the help of local artists. Other students prepare skits for their own participation in the program. The school publications and publicity office turns out publicity materials. The television program committee plans similarly.

Some of the young people from the "eyesore" area are assigned the responsibility of getting their parents to participate in a bazaar in the streets adjacent to the school. Stands are set up for the display, and for the sale of representative foods, art objects, colorful garments and the like. The school gymnasium is reserved for a folk-dancing festival. Skillfully prepared posters and materials calling attention to the program to make the community a more beautiful place in which to live are available for all to see and read. Clergymen, reached through the Community Council, preach appropriate sermons. Multilingual literature spreads the appeals.

Mr. Marchetti, too, plays his part. Encouraged by his experiences with young people to whom he gives part-time employment in his flower shop, Mr. Marchetti sets up simple floral displays throughout the community to indicate what flowers and growing plants can do for community appearance. During the evenings he becomes a consulting expert for community residents, with headquarters in the horticulture classes of the school.

Almost imperceptibly at first, but with rapidly increasing momentum, most citizens of Midvale take hold of the campaign. Thus, on one of his local walks, Joe Roberts is delighted to see groups of neighbors discussing ways and means of enhancing the attractiveness of their blocks. On one street, Mr. Mars, the owner of two buildings, has had the exteriors freshly painted and adorned with colorful tiles. On another block, Joe is invited by an obviously "about-to-spring-a-surprise" group to come through the hallway of their house into the back yard. There Joe notices that not only have new gardens been planted, but the residents of several adjacent houses have torn down the fences dividing their back yards, and have run a continuous flower garden for three-quarters of the block. As Mrs. Murphy puts it, "Even the kids are having a grand time together as they clear out the weeds."

One day, the manager of a local department store is approached by a number of citizens. "We've come," says Mrs. Torres, "to ask whether you and the other merchants in our community could give us some ideas on making our apartments look better. We were wondering whether you could use the school auditorium to put on some displays and demonstrations of different possible arrangements we could use. Some of us would like to offer suggestions that we've used to make our own places more livable. In that way, we could get many ideas and make up our own minds as to what to do."

And so the stores came to Midvale High's auditorium for a home decoration clinic. The interior decorators had to earn their spurs. Many were the questions as to "whys," "how much," and "how about this?" Because of the enthusiasm generated, many stores offered the services of visiting employees to help residents plan improvements for their own homes.

What delights so many of the people of Midvale about all this is the discovery that many of their neighbors have abilities and contributions which can be shared. Mrs. Simmons discovers that paintings can brighten up a home. When she discusses her eagerness to have some for her apartment, and her despair at not being able to afford any, Mr. Nichello recommends that she join the Midvale evening art class and learn to paint for herself. To her own amazement, Mrs. Simmons finds that surrounded by other folk like herself who share mutual problems and enthusiasms, she develops a keen eye for color, and an ability for self-expression on canvas. When she hangs her first picture on her wall, Mrs.

Simmons has the neighbors in for their applause. Before she knows it, Mrs. Simmons is being invited in by Mrs. Smith and others for her opinions on their home decorations. She is asked to display her paintings at the annual five-day outdoor community art exhibit held in the playlots which have been cleared and made available by community residents for recreation purposes.

In all this bustle to make Midvale the community beautiful in the city beautiful, the faculty of Midvale High plays an active role. Small wonder this, for the Midvale faculty is a community resources staff. It is composed of a regular full-time staff, and community part-time assistants.

Community Resources Staff

The full-time staff is the result of a careful system of preparation and selection. To assist in this task, the State Colleges and Teacher-Education Institutes have moved away from a stress on preparing subject-matter specialists, who think of education largely as learning which is centered in logically organized subject-fields. Instead, the emphasis in the five years of preparation is on the application of knowledge to the solution of problems, in developing an understanding of cultural patterns of different groups as in Metropolita, and in affording maximum experiences in community activity and the group process. In addition, they receive a thorough grounding in specialized fields of knowledge. Thus, a would-be mathematics expert learns not only mathematical theory but the applications to life problems in practical mathematics and consumer education. All teaching candidates then serve a year's apprenticeship with pay, followed by one or two additional years of professional preparation in an approved university or teachers college anywhere in the world. This enables each teaching candidate to show what he can do and learn, and to indicate to the guidance and selection staff his ability to work toward the objectives of the community education program. Final selection is made by a special committee composed of his school principals, two teachers, two parents, two students, and two members of the community at large. In this selection an attempt is made to balance numbers among residents and nonresidents of the community so as to assure both local and fresh viewpoints.

No teacher is assigned to more than six hours of school responsibilities a day. Specific assignments are made which may combine teaching of youngsters and adults, guidance, community work, committee work, or administrative work. A teacher obviously may not do all of these things in any one period of time.

In addition, every member of the staff is allotted one hour daily for personal professional improvement. This time can be used to study professional reports and literature, to observe the work of others, to attend courses or conferences, do independent community research, and the like.

Every classroom is equipped with a combination office-workroom so that the teacher can have a place to do his own work and to keep needed instructional materials close at hand. When a teacher engages in such community work as assisting in the publication of the school-community newspaper, addressing community clubs, supervising out-of-school work of youngsters, he can thus invite community people to his own office for informal meetings. Every effort is made to assure the instructor of the means required to pursue the cultural, professional, recreational, and educational experiences necessary for his growth. Beginning salaries are high enough to attract capable newcomers, while experienced teachers of demonstrated ability receive salaries equal to those paid leaders in law, medicine, and government.

In their instructional work, teachers are encouraged to utilize community resource people, surveys and field trips, participation in civic service projects, student planning and evaluation, an abundance of audio-visual materials, and to develop that warm co-operative spirit which grows out of face-to-face, informal, working together.

It has been found that certain citizens make such a contribution to the educational program that many of them are invited, as Mr. Marchetti was, to become informal community members of the staff. Such citizen-teachers have introduced many worthwhile innovations in instructional methods and techniques in the areas of their special competence.

Partners in Common Efforts

As Midvale High engages more and more young people, adults, and staff members in the drive for colorful living, certain special problems of the Midvale community become apparent. Because of population congestion, Sanitation Department pickups are falling behind community need. Immigration, as well as migration from other sections of the country into Midvale, produce housing shortages which add to the congestion, and waste disposal facilities required by law are inadequate. It becomes obvious to the school-community committee, and in turn to the Midvale Council, that special steps will have to be taken before the colorful-living campaign can be a success. Contact is made with the Metropolita Citizens' Council. The Commissioner of Sanitation is invited to a special Midvale meeting to explain whether pickup facilities can be improved within the framework of Metropolita's resources. When the statistics gathered by students make clear the evident urgency in Midvale, the Commissioner arranges Department services to meet Midvale's request.

Again, the Commissioners of Health and Buildings are called to the Midvale Community to meet with local political leaders and other citizens to consider what can be done to increase waste-disposal facilities. Frank Rodriguez, the boy who hopes to be a lawyer some day, proposes that the Sanitary Code of Metropolita be amended to require provision by landlords of additional garbage cans. The assembled experts concur and a revised code is drafted.

Reports of Midvale's efforts, and of those from other Metropolita communities, go to the Metropolita Council. Slogans and suggestions for effective procedures to enhance the quality of community life are distributed.

As all Metropolita becomes increasingly stirred over ways to make life in a great city more restful, more beautiful, the Metropolita Council announces that it will create and award city certificates of distinguished civic service to those communities which show the most improvement in a community project each year. This year's awards are to be made on the basis of "colorful living" achievement.

Midvale, already at full steam, now increases its civic effort. Block committees check and recheck block appearance. Student meetings exchange ideas. The school horticulture classes, with the aid of the bustling Mr. Marchetti, turn out flowers and plants galore. The school and community press calls attention to progress and to areas requiring further attention, sound truck appeals are made for maximum efforts, the school radio and television stations coin slogans and recommend patterns of improved home decoration, and parents spend time with the school art department for assistance in crystalizing their own ideas most effectively.

Every community council in the city meets to appraise and evaluate the efforts in the local communities to measure gains in appearance and lessons in community cooperation. Reports go to the Metropolita Council.

On the basis of these reports and on the basis of direct inspections by members of the Metropolita Council, the first award for outstanding achievement is given to the Midvale Community. At the Council meeting which makes the presentation of the "Distinguished Community Service Certificate" to Joe Roberts, representing Midvale, there is a general glow of civic pride. All the people of Metropolita feel membership in community and city, partners in common efforts for improved living.

In the very midst of self-congratulations on the campaign, other delegates arise to point the way to new efforts. Mike Raines, labor leader, stands up to call attention to another problem, newly arisen in Metropolita. "Ladies and Gentlemen," he begins, ". . . . .

2

Implications

Education in any culture reflects the values inherent in that culture. This fact is clearly apparent when we look at educational systems different from our own. The Western world is all too familiar with fascist educational institutions which marshaled all educational resources for the promotion of ideals of racial superiority, the glorification of war and of the State. We are now witnessing the power of communist educational institutions which also stress the importance of the State along with suspicion and hatred of all noncommunist peoples. Both systems consciously utilize education as an instrument for training young and old in the accepted ideology.

In the United States we do not believe in the dominance of education by the State. Here the principle of individual freedom allows local communities to develop varying types of educational programs. This is a unique characteristic of American education. It has made possible a rich diversification of experimental effort, unsurpassed by any country of the world. But freedom with us has also made possible the continuance of archaic educational institutions which promote authoritarian values much nearer fascism than democracy.

In this welter of conflicting purposes and educational practices community education emerges as perhaps the most promising type of educational practice for the promotion of democratic values. Its peculiar strength arises from its emphasis upon the participation of children, youth, adults, and community institutions in the co-operative task of education. It assumes a dynamic growth in local communities, and in society, which seeks to move toward a more democratic social order. If this is not the orientation of all community educational ventures it is, at least, the conception accepted by the contributors to Part I.

SCHOOL AND COMMUNITY RELATIONSHIPS

It is no accident that the three imaginary programs—rural, small town and city—start with descriptions of the nature of local communities. Schools of the conventional pattern are much alike—east, west, north and south—for they have been oriented to the teaching of skills and knowledges which are relatively unrelated to local needs. But every *community education* program must be unique, as these three programs are unique, for they are the warp and woof of the community life. Where the economic and social patterns differ the schools will differ, in administration, organization, and specific curriculum content. Community schools, of the American pattern, have this in common, however: they accept, and seek to achieve, the basic democratic ideals of respect for the individual person, active participation of learners in the improvement of the conditions of the common life, and continuous experimentation and evaluation of results.

The close integration of school and community is especially well shown in the case of the "Visby" school. In order that truly democratic values be implemented the author has envisaged a community somewhat different in social morés from that commonly found in American life. People will differ as to the desirability of such community structure. But the basic assumption, that school and community are continually remaking each other through an interactive process, is apparent and valid.

"Timber Lake" and "Metropolita" are more conventional in basic design. Unlike the Visby rural program, the Timber Lake pattern with its school district reorganization "brought all outlying rural districts into the Timber Lake Community School." Metropolita developed in one of our great cities, largely centers in a school plant. It is, however, closely related to a city area-wide organization where co-operative plans are developed for integrating many local community programs in a city comprising millions of people.

In all three cases, it is assumed that the power factors of the community—especially those involving business, labor and religion—have recognized the basic values of this community approach to education, and have supported (or at least permitted) these developments to occur. Since these and many other social groupings nominally, at least, support "education for democracy," they all can co-operate in effective community education.

LEADERSHIP AND PERSONNEL

In the programs described "teachers are, first of all, human beings, then citizens, then teachers." They are well paid and carefully selected for the types of tasks to be performed. In a very real sense each supporting community is "educational-centered." Teachers are representative of various racial and ethnic groups.

> Community members are proud that they (the teachers) represent several races and groups, including Negro, Indian, Hindu and Japanese, for Visby believes that we cannot be one world until the principles underlying countries such as theirs are universally adopted.

In the larger sense, all citizens have educational functions to perform and therefore may be thought of as teachers. Participants vary from the director of a commercial enterprise to a housewife who demonstrates the best way to can fruit; from the chairman of a Community Council to a high school boy who reports in a study of local unsanitary conditions that "people often pitch garbage out of their windows"; from Mr. Marchetti, a local florist, to an assemblyman in the local school district.

In community education all citizens are teachers or potential teachers, as well as learners. They give of their expertness in an interrelated living process, and by so doing, become active agents in the educational process of community improvement.

In building the school-community life leadership is important. Some one individual may be instrumental in setting the stage and furnishing the initial motive power. In Timber Lake a new superintendent of schools got things under way. In Metropolita the educational program of the city was organized on a community basis as the result of a sociological study involving many persons. But the democratic test of leadership is in the number and variety of leaders. The acid test is found in what happens when one or more of the motivating personalities is removed from the situation. Do others assume their roles? Does the effective school community process go on to new achievements and new problems? Our imaginative accounts described at one moment in time do not, and cannot, give us the answer to such questions as these.

CURRICULUM AND PROGRAM

Community-oriented educational programs are motivated by a vision of a better community and society than now exist. The dynamic response which is called forth by programs and plans for a finer life is part of the American dream. The vision of a finer tomorrow is the life-blood of community education. When Joe Roberts, the high school principal, spoke to his fellow citizens who are participants in building an educational program, he appealed to the dynamic drive of Americans toward a better tomorrow.

In a community program the curriculum is in a constant process of change to meet the needs of the participants. The process involves group interaction. Children, youth, parents, citizens are continually engaged in solving problems which arise in the common process of education and community living. The comparative rigidity of the conventional school curricula, which is academic in orientation, determined in advance and not by the learners, is completely foreign to the type of social interaction we are here exploring.

Curriculum building in a community program involves all learners—teachers, pupils and citizens—in the use of the problem-solving method of learning. Using the group process, purposes are clarified, problems are analyzed, data are collected, lines of action agreed upon, action taken, results evaluated, and new hypotheses accepted for further action.

Illustrations of this group problem-solving process are found in different stages of development in the three imaginative programs.

John's core group had been considering, "Housing Needs in Our Community." They now intensify their efforts. They make maps of land use, investigate land values and compile statistics on average incomes. John finds himself interviewing tenants and landlords on living facilities, apartment beautification, street appearance, and the like. With the help of the Midvale Community Advisory Council, the class is enabled to hear members of the City Planning Commission. They proceed to write letters to local political, civic, business, and religious leaders urging effective action. With the help of the art staff, they build models of the kind of community they would like to live in, and invite architects and planning engineers to appraise their efforts. Displays of student ceramics and shop work, which could be used in homes, are set up in the windows of many local stores.

The joint planning necessary in community education is well described in the Timber Lake account:

Committees which are broadly representative of the school and the people operate as creative working groups. It is one of these committees which recently gained national recognition for its curriculum in home and family living, a program which has stood up under vigorous evaluation.

Another working group, in cooperation with the Timber Lake Community Council and the high school and community college classes in social relationships, has explored the economic resources, job opportunities, and labor supply of the community and the region. Their findings have served as a guide for education for economic competence. This program includes vocational guidance and exploration, on-the-job training and numerous group projects in homemaking, agriculture and conservation, consumer education and the management of a marketing cooperative.

Timber Lake's Committee on Human Relations has recently been engaged in an ambitious project in group dynamics. It has attempted to define the role of administrators, teachers, parents, and students in school and community life.

Instruction in the Visby School is described as:

Informal always, but it is not haphazard. In organization it becomes increasingly logical just as the mind itself does (in problem solving). In this there is no force. Groups form to seek a systematic understanding in one field or another. They dissolve when that purpose is met.

Youth carries its part in an exhaustive study of natural resources—in minerals, in flora, in fauna, in sources of energy. Daily experience is habitually analyzed for problems needing scientific inquiry. In a number of homes in Visby are to be found science laboratories of surprising equipment and activity. Some of these are maintained by secondary school students; some are operated jointly by companions; several are distinctly family enterprises where mother, father, and several children find delight in pooling their inventiveness in furthering experiments.

All this is in strong contrast to the so-called textbook "experiments" in which the "pupil" follows routine directions to almost inevitable conclusions. One sees the results of such an approach to science in the alertness of the citizens in meeting the problems of home, farm, village.

In this community-problem-solving type of education pertinent research materials are made easily available.

If there is one central building of the school plant, it is the library, or more properly, the "materials bureau." Here one finds no endless collection of ancient books and textbooks. Instead there is a functional collection of the most modern treatments in each field. Older books, with suitable exceptions, are obtained when needed from the state library. The Bureau circulates its own collection of films, slides, charts, pictures, models, recordings and transcriptions, including the best in music, language courses, and lectures. There are scientific exhibits. Special rooms within the library are set aside for the use of individuals and groups at study. Such rooms of varying size and type of furniture and equipment replace the usual school classrooms.

Each of the three reports makes provision for a "Materials Bureau," a "Science Hall," "Learning Resources Center" or "Laboratory for Life Studies." The real laboratory, in each case, however, is the particular community and society in which the school functions. Here are to be found the problems which need solution, as well as the data which must be analyzed and evaluated before even tentative solutions can be found. Laboratory facilities—the "bookmobile" in one of the plans—merely expedite the process.

It is apparent in the three programs that, unlike the traditional school which gets its organization from academic subjects, community education is clearly oriented toward helping people solve real problems in the various areas of modern living. In the words of one of the authors, these areas include "making a living, utilizing natural resources, maintaining a home, sharing in citizenship, securing an education, maintaining health, worshipping, enjoying leisure time and building good human relationships."

In recent years many professional reports—notably the *Seven Cardinal Principles of Secondary Education* (1918), the *Purposes of Education in American Democracy* (1938), *Education for All American Youth* (1944, 1952) and *Education for All American Children* (1948), and *Life Adjustment Education*—have stressed the importance of educating in and for the basic areas of social living. Yet all too few schools and communities have made the changes in curriculum content and organization implicit in such reports. The reorientation required is a most difficult hurdle for the conventional professional and lay mind. Conventional minds find it very difficult to escape the old-world orientation of academic scholarly subjects, perpetuated, as they have been, by traditional American schools and colleges.

The curriculum plans here idealized accept the new orientation. The school is seen as moving into educational action to help improve the quality of community life. Educational institutions are thus given new and creative functions to perform. Health and employment centers, baby clinics, radio and neighborhood recreation facilities, headquarters of research and community planning—all are integrally related to the educational plant and the educational program.

In one notable respect our three imaginative plans go far beyond the type of "community school" envisaged a brief decade and a half ago.[1] Earlier thinking and practice did not adequately relate education for local community living to education for the national and world community. The impact of two world wars has raised our eyes from contemplation of what is immediately about us to the realization that we are actually living in one technological world, though social institutions are largely operating as if we were not.

Modern community education seeks to educate for one world, just as all realistic social institutions must seek this desired end. The clear alternative is the continuance of war and threats of war.

All three plans are concerned with the development of educational programs which accept, as first class American citizens, people of all races, nationalities and religions—Japanese and Mexican Americans, Negroes, Puerto Ricans, newly arrived immigrants. This is a necessary step in the development of world citizenship.

The programs also suggest many educational experiences intended to raise our eyes from the local to the world scene. The study of what is happening in England, Germany, India, Canada, The Union of South Africa; the exchange of teachers with foreign lands; the exchange of

[1] Samuel Everett, ed. *The Community School* (New York: D. Appleton-Century, 1938).

students; teacher and student travel abroad; the utilization of foreign visitors in the educational process; participation in foreign relief projects; the "adoption" of a foreign community are among the specific methods suggested.

PERSPECTIVE

In a very real sense the foregoing analysis has been also an evaluation of the three imaginative community school programs. The reports themselves contain emphases which will seem wise, or unwise, according to each reader's own professional and social frame of reference. And that is exactly as it should be, since all of these programs represent extensions beyond anything that now exists. As already stated, these descriptions are presented to stimulate thinking and to provoke comment, as well as to suggest desirable directions of school-and-community program development. Let us now turn to some existing practice, to advances already actually made by operating American schools. This we shall do in Part II.

PART

II

These Schools Are Moving Ahead

Part I has sketched broadly the kind of school program which the Committee believes to be imperative in rural regions, towns and cities. Part II now reports some of the techniques and procedures which actual, existing American school systems have already successfully used in developing community school programs. Analysis of these twelve selected case studies indicates clearly that the community-type school program is both practical and promising at all age levels.

3

Getting Started

Many people — teachers, parents, school supervisors and administrators, board of education members—accept the basic philosophy of the community school. They are sincerely interested in "linking education with life," in making "the learning process both practical and meaningful," in "using education to improve the quality of living"—in short, in developing conventional schools into true community schools. Moreover, they are willing to begin on any level of activity. They confess, however, that they lack sufficient "know-how." They want to learn how to begin, where and how to take hold of the community education idea, and how to move forward with it. Yet successful community school teachers and administrators often do not recall the smaller ways in which they began, nor even how they moved forward from first beginnings. When asked about their procedures, they are likely as not to say: "Oh, I just started where I was, and used what was close at hand." Such answers seem to make community education almost a matter of inspiration, of unplanned improvising. Since this is not the way to develop a community school, the present chapter describes reports from schools which have been successful in school-community activities, with special attention to the procedures used in getting them started.

Apparently community schools never "just happen." They are caused by an interaction of forces within the community, and by the emergence of a leader, or leaders, either native to the locality or adopted by it. Community schools are begun by many types of people, and in many different ways. There seems to be no clear-cut pattern of who begins "the community idea" in schools, nor of the activities which launch the movement to implement the idea in daily practice. Sometimes community-school programs are started by teachers and children; often they reflect the efforts of school administrators, supervisors, or consultants; frequently they are initiated by the work of parents and other interested lay people; occasionally they reflect the efforts of university or state department of education. One of the most intriguing aspects of community education is that anybody concerned about people and the responsibilities of education in a democratic society can help to launch and expand the community school idea in his own area.

TENANT PLUS KNOW-HOW
EQUALS OWNER [1]

At Pilot Point, Texas, there is a rural, consolidated school to which an individual citizen of the community appealed for help. This is the story of the help he received, what it did for him personally, and how it helped tie the school and its community more closely together.

Pilot Point is a farming community of 1,100 people, some twenty miles from Denton, Texas. Prosperity there depends in large part upon intelligent use of the land.

[1] Reported in *Applied Economics for Better Living*, 3:2-3; June, 1949.

Conscious of this basic fact, the Pilot Point school had for some years participated in the project called "Applied Economics for Better Living," sponsored nationally by the American Association of Colleges for Teacher Education.

Then Albert Duessman rented a farm on the outskirts of Pilot Point. The land was poor, and badly eroded by water and by wind. Along the fence lines the drifts of soil had piled up two and three feet high, a sure sign that many tons of it had been blown entirely away. The lifeless top soil that was left greatly needed nourishment.

Mr. Duessman was young and a good worker, but these characteristics are not enough when the land is poor. By working hard the first year Mr. Duessman managed to produce 10 to 15 bushels of peanuts per acre, 10 bushels of corn, and a little cotton. Disaster lies in such meager results; they spell nothing but poverty, struggle, and disappointment. The next step Mr. Duessman took indicated that he had intelligence as well as youth and energy. He knew where to look for help, and he sought it. He went to Porter G. Gentry, the Vocational Agriculture teacher at the Pilot Point School, for advice.

Mr. Gentry not only advised, he also brought his high-school class to the farm and demonstrated both to the class and to Mr. Duessman what ought to be done to the land. First essentials, he said, were terraces to prevent water erosion, and winter cover-crops to stop wind erosion and, when plowed under, to enrich the soil. The boys in the class ran some terraces—serpentine mounds of earth about two feet high and eight feet wide running at intervals along the contour to control the flow of rain water—to show how it was done.

Mr. Duessman followed the teacher's advice, which was backed up by that of the local soil conservationist. Fortunately the soil was loose and sandy, well suited to peanuts, and responded to good treatment much more rapidly than the heavier soil a few miles north.

The results were spectacular. In six years Mr. Duessman quintupled his production of peanuts and corn and tripled his production of cotton. When the delegates to the Applied Economics Conference (then meeting at the North Texas State College at Denton) visited him, he was on his tractor running a terrace with a special attachment which did the job quickly and efficiently. He had not only bought the farm and added new equipment, but had built himself a new brick house with a deep-freeze unit, an ultramodern kitchen, and had a new car in the garage.

It is of course true that most teachers are not as advantageously placed as the vocational agriculture teacher in respect to making a direct contribution to better living. But it seems that the teachers of any subject, if they set out to do it, could make equal if sometimes less direct or immediately striking contributions to the improvement of life in their own communities.

A FIFTH GRADE EXAMINES
LIVING COSTS [2]

Sometimes the interest of children in community affairs is stimulated by the use of current and local curriculum materials. If the children become genuinely concerned about their findings, and have competent assistance in making their analysis, desirable social action may follow.

[2] Reported by Doris MacGregor, teacher in the Bailey School, Springfield, Missouri.

GETTING STARTED 63

The "high cost of living" is not a problem peculiar to
adults. It operates also in the lives of middle-grade children who hear the problem discussed by their parents and
are also troubled by it. Because facing facts is good mental
hygiene, it is the duty of adults—parents and teachers alike
—to help children understand what is happening in the
world about them.

From the beginning of the year, the fifth-graders in the
Ed V. William School at Springfield, Missouri, had been
asking questions about the high cost of living. "What makes
food so high?" "What will happen to us this winter?" "Will
there be food enough to last all winter?" "What will happen if my Daddy loses his job?"

The twins in the room found comfort in their home environment. "Well, we'll not go hungry if our Daddy does
lose his job because we have a pig, a cow, chickens, and a
cellar full of food we canned from our garden." Others
spoke, but not with such confidence. Discussion on the high
cost of living was so frequent and so serious that the teacher
decided it was a problem of real concern to most of the
fifth graders, and so should be faced by them.

Getting the Facts

The first step was to ask the children to gather news items
about the high cost of living from the newspapers, to discuss
the matter with their parents, and to listen to radio broadcasts on the subject. At first, contributions were meager and
slight, but interest begets interest, and soon clippings, car-
toons, and whole newspapers began piling up in the school
room. These resources became real learning materials. To
read a newspaper intelligently and to interpret accurately
what one reads is an achievement, whether the reader be
twelve or forty. Out of reading came discussion and from

this sharing emerged the problems: (1) What are the causes of high prices? (2) How can prices be brought down? and (3) How do high prices affect people? First they found basic questions, then sought for the answers.

The group set to work on answers to the above questions. Magazines were used to supplement newspapers, discussions followed, and scrapbooks developed. Interestingly enough, the children became fascinated with graphs. One committee searching for answers to their questions found a graph in a magazine which gave meaning to the term "basic crop" and to the importance of grain. The children enlarged the graph, reproduced it on a chart, and used it to illustrate how edible products can be obtained by feeding grain, as for example one bushel of wheat produces $4\frac{3}{4}$ pounds of beef. One child developed a graph of the Food Dollar, illustrating through shading its reduced value. Others were developed to show production and prices, and supply and demand. Many original ideas were suggested by a child who had difficulty in reading. He listened attentively to discussions and one day remarked: "That's like two elevators going up and down." "Yes, it is," said the teacher. "Suppose you illustrate the idea." "By myself?" asked the child. "You may choose anyone you wish," replied the teacher, and he did—one of the bright and capable ones. Together the children produced an excellent piece of work, using pulleys, a block of wood, and weights. Here was visual education in effective action!

Someone discovered that the children in the fourth grade were studying "Food and Its Relationship to Health," and suggested that they might have something of value to share with the children in the fifth grade. As a result of conferences the fifth grade children visited those in the fourth, and three films on the production, distribution and consumption of food were shared by the children.

Organizing the Findings

One cannot collect information and share it in groups very long without facing the necessity of its organization into some sort of form. The following list shows how this was accomplished through a break-down of the original questions.

A. *Some reasons for high prices:*
1. Production shortages
2. Speculation on food products
3. Wastefulness and carelessness of the people
4. Public acceptance of high prices
5. Share products with other countries
6. Unfavorable weather
7. Increased population
8. Destruction by rats

B. *Some things we can do to bring prices down:*
1. Buyer's strike
2. Stopping wastefulness
3. Volunteering to eat less
4. Consumer co-operatives
5. Ceiling prices
6. Rationing
7. Producing more

C. *Ways high prices affect us:*
1. Bad for health
2. Reduces the pocketbook
3. Keeps people from having many of the necessary things
4. It causes wages to go up
5. It causes people to be afraid

As one might expect, the children were not equally enthusiastic about all phases of their study. They were challenged to find that wastefulness and carelessness on the part of large numbers of American people—even in families like their own—was a factor contributing to high prices. This, too, might be expected since children are quick to see things they can do though they are not necessarily willing to follow a consistent line of action. "What can we do about wastefulness and carelessness?" asked the teacher. "Stop wasting," the children replied with characteristic forthrightness. When they considered how they might help, the problem of wasting food at the noon lunch period came up for discussion. The teacher wondered about the effectiveness of their reasoning in regard to this problem, but was gratified to note some improvement in saving foods at the noon hour.

Taking Action

The concluding phase of the whole study probably afforded most satisfaction to both pupils and teacher. It grew out of considering ways to share what America had with other countries and how feelings of insecurity caused by high prices might be resolved. One suggestion brought before the group by the teacher was the formation of consumer co-operatives. She suggested that the group might set up one of their own and learn from actual experience some of the values of such an enterprise. The children seemed interested at first. That they were more co-operative than interested, however, soon became apparent when another opportunity for sharing came to their attention.

In *The Young Citizen*, a school newspaper to which the group subscribes, the children had found several articles dealing with the food situation at home and abroad. Local city newspapers had been publishing a series of sensational stories dealing with two districts outside the city limits, whose residents were undernourished, scantily clothed, and poorly housed. One youngster expressed concern, "Why do we have to help the people in Europe when the people in Springfield are hungry?" Another replied, "Yes, but we must remember those people in Europe suffered in the war for us." After discussing both comments the group decided that it must share what it had with those people living in the devastated countries as well as with those at home.

One article in *The Young Citizen* had explained how groups might have a share in helping people in the war-devastated countries by contributing money to be administered for foreign relief through the special organization CARE. The group listed reasons why they thought this would be a good thing to do:

1. CARE is a nonprofit organization
2. CARE is one of the foreign relief plans
3. CARE gives us a chance to help other people
4. CARE helps to make friends

Here was a concern that had reality for these children. The teacher recognized that the idea had values beyond those which might be gained from an experience with a co-operative venture in their own classroom. For one thing, the children were more interested in helping others than they were in helping themselves. The teacher followed their lead, though she had misgivings that the $10 required to participate in CARE could be raised by them.

The suggestion for taking part in a project for CARE had come from a few children, but the teacher soon saw that the idea was accepted by the group. They wanted to do something to help others meet the serious problems of living today. They wanted their money used for a family with children near their own ages. They hoped they might get letters from these children, which they vowed they would answer promptly.

The practical question of the $10 gave everybody concern. How could a fifth-grade group of children raise the necessary amount? Could enthusiasm surmount the difficulties? The children began by listing four methods to raise the money:

1. Find work to do
2. Have a popsicle sale
3. Bring in money from allowances
4. Take an offering at PTA to give the mothers an opportunity to share

These were not idle suggestions. All four actually yielded financial aid. Much of the success of the group was due to the persistence of its dynamic chairman. Each day he tactfully reminded the children of suggestions 1 and 3 on their list. And each day the fund grew. Emphasis was placed on voluntary contributions. No amount was set, even as a goal for individuals. Pennies and nickels were as happily received as larger amounts. One child earned seventy-five cents and gave all of it. Another proudly contributed his nickel. A popsicle sale planned and carried out by the group netted only sixty cents. This was disappointing, but the group had had a good experience: they learned that popsicle sales in November are not apt to be profitable. The PTA contributions to the fund surprised and thrilled the children. They had planned a program for the November PTA meeting to tell their mothers about the problems they were studying. As a part of this program they gave an opportunity for the mothers to share in raising their fund. When the coins were counted, the children were amazed to find they totaled $3.87, bringing their fund to more than $8, and practically assuring success for the undertaking.

When the $10 was finally achieved, the group enjoyed a busy planning-and-working period, getting their letter written to CARE, learning about money orders, and choosing a committee to visit the nearby branch post office to purchase their money order.

This last phase seemed an appropriate climax to the study of the high cost of living for the fifth-grade children. They had built up a fund of information about the reasons for high prices and ways for lowering them. They had gained some understanding of how high prices affect the lives of all people and the need for help in controlling them. They had developed new respect for two important factors affecting food supplies and prices—the farmer, who is chiefly responsible for production, and the weather, which both hinders and helps the farmer. These two new ideas were so challenging to the group that it was anticipated that the next problem would probably deal with both. However, prices will no doubt continue to be a subject of interest, since they will go on affecting daily living, and because the children have become sensitive to radio and press comments in regard to what is being done about them.

As the teacher evaluated the study she considered one bit of evidence as important. Christmas parties, with an exchange of gifts among pupils, are the usual pre-holiday celebration in the Ed V. William School. The year of the study of the high cost of living the fifth-grade children of their own accord chose to forego the usual party so as to pool their gift money and present it to the Children's Home in the city. The children through voluntary contributions collected $6, and once more proved to themselves that satisfactions are to be had from helping others.

COLLEGE STUDENTS
ENTER POLITICS [3]

The citizen today, in a society dominated by vast and impersonal forces, is faced with a prodigious task. He may be so bewildered by the complex world in which he lives that he will be tempted to stand by helplessly, accepting the kind of a society that fate imposes, rather than feeling an individual responsibility to do something about that society. A good way to combat such a fatalistic attitude and to furnish an emotional incentive to action is to provide laboratory experience in civic participation as part of the educational process. Here is how this was done by the Maxwell School of Citizenship and Public Affairs at Syracuse University.

For too long it has been taken for granted that the will to participate in community affairs would follow automatically from knowledge gained from books or classroom lectures and discussions. College educators, in particular, have lost sight of the fact that citizen participation is often emotionally motivated, and such motivation is more likely to be developed through actual experience than through secondhand contacts in the classroom or in reading materials. Educational experts have been telling us for many years that the most effective way to learn is by "doing," and the natural sciences have based their teaching techniques on this principle. Such laboratory methods, however,

[3] Reported by Marguerite J. Fisher, "The Community as a Laboratory in General Education." *School and Society*, 73:151-153, March 10, 1951.

are not generally utilized in college training in citizenship. Instead, students are too often bombarded by preachments and exhortations which fall on sterile soil because of the failure to inculcate a drive to action through genuine experience.

In an undergraduate course designed for junior and senior students in the Maxwell School of Citizenship and Public Affairs at Syracuse University, an effort has been made to provide such practical citizenship experience and to help the student span the gap between the printed word and reality. In addition to readings and lectures, during the year the students take part in a series of laboratory experiences in as many fields of community participation as are feasible.

Political Party Activity

The first series of projects is designed to furnish first-hand insight and experience in political party activities. Each student is required to do twelve hours of actual political-party work during the October campaign. After choosing the party in which he wishes to work, the student is turned over to a local party official, usually an election-district committeeman or committeewoman. These party officials are informed about the purpose of the project and are willing to use the students as their assistants. The twelve hours of work must be divided roughly as follows: six hours at the polls on registration days and on election day, three hours of canvassing or "doorbell ringing" in the election districts, and three hours at party headquarters. Such personal experience is indeed the base for realistic leaning.

The tasks assigned to the students are left to the discretion of the party officials, with the stipulation that this is not to be "made-work," but genuine party activity. For example, on registration and election days the students sit in the polling places, checking off on master lists the names of party members as they come in to vote. Some students call recalcitrant citizens on the telephone, reminding them that they have not voted; others pass out leaflets and campaign materials. In some cases the students have driven cars to transport voters to and from the polls.

In house-to-house canvassing the students are often as successful as the more seasoned party workers. The apprentice canvassers meet in advance with a party official who coaches them in the accepted techniques. At party headquarters, the students make their appearance at times when the local officials have requested their assistance. They are assigned to various useful tasks which include answering telephones, delivering messages, running errands, addressing envelopes, serving as receptionists, and demonstrating the voting machines.

Campaigns and Rallies

As a second project in their training in practical politics, the students are required to attend and report on four campaign meetings or political rallies, not more than two of which may be in one party. In their written reports on these meetings the students evaluate the political speeches and campaign arguments. Since Syracuse is a large city, there is at least one major rally staged by each party during the campaign, at which time some celebrity such as a gubernatorial or senatorial candidate makes his appearance. Through their attendance at these rallies the students have the opportunity not only to meet and study campaign personalities, but to recognize and analyze various types of political appeals and propaganda.

Government Offices

In a third series of projects the students undertake some citizen participation in governmental administration in the local community. The projects here have varied from year to year, depending on the policies emphasized in the various city and county agencies. In a recent project the students undertook for the benefit of the local recreation department a survey of the leisure-time activities of some 150 representative citizens. The survey covered such matters as the activities most frequently engaged in during leisure time and the kinds of recreation in which the individual would most like to participate if the opportunity were available. The results of the survey were then used by the local government as a basis in evaluating its recreation facilities.

Civic Organizations

The fourth series of projects brings the students into contact with civic organizations in the local community. The American Legion, the Kiwanis Club, and other groups have proved co-operative in giving the students genuine experience in civic activity. This year the League of Women Voters found useful work for the students in connection with its statewide campaign for a law for permanent registration of voters. The League decided to make a study of nonvoters in order to secure evidence to present to the state legislature when its permanent registration law was introduced. It was anticipated that interviews with nonvoters would reveal that most of the reasons for failure to vote would be eliminated under the permanent registration system advocated by the League. Throughout New York State,

League members interviewed thousands of nonvoters after the registration period was over. In Syracuse the students carried the burden of this task, interviewing over 400 nonvoters whom they found through a door-to-door canvass. The evidence turned up by the students bore out the League's expectations and will be used in support of the League's permanent registration law when it is introduced in the state legislature.

Social-welfare Agencies

A fifth series of projects introduces the students to the manifold activities carried on by the social-welfare agencies of the local community. The students are sent, in small groups, to the agencies providing services for children, sick or disabled persons, and the mentally ill, or to those agencies operating in the fields of family welfare, housing, recreation, or health protection. Most of these agencies have numerous volunteer jobs. Their needs generally outnumber the volunteers available. These needs are as varied as the personalities and backgrounds of the students, and for everyone there is some kind of volunteer work which holds a special interest and in which the individual can use his abilities in a way that will benefit the community. Recently, one group of students helped in the program of a community recreation center; another group taught classes in the juvenile detention home; still another group organized leisure-time activities for the aged at the county home.

Through these volunteer activities not only do the students gain the benefits of actual citizen participation, but, in addition, they obtain a firsthand insight into the social problems and human needs in the local community. Furthermore, they become acquainted with the various agencies and groups which are trying to meet these needs. Knowledge gained in this way is far more meaningful than a description of social welfare agencies encountered on the written page or even in the instructor's lecture.

PROBLEM-SOLVING
IN COMMUNITY STUDY [4]

Community education may well begin right at home— in the school community itself. This is an account showing how the problem-solving method was utilized by fourth-grade children studying their own community. Valuable as this report on method is, it is still more significant because the project finally involved the school community as well as its fourth-grade children.

This project concentrated upon developing community sensitivity in fourth-grade children of average intelligence. The problem-solving method was deliberately used throughout. These steps in that method were first identified by the teacher for her own guidance:

1. Clarifying the problem
2. Gathering the evidence
3. Organizing the facts
4. Drawing tentative conclusions
5. Going into action
6. Evaluating the results

It should be remembered, however, that the steps outlined above are not mutually exclusive. No single part of

[4] Reported by Sadie K. Zion, teacher of grade 4, James L. Ludlow School, Philadelphia, Pennsylvania.

the problem-solving process takes place by itself at a given time. Some part of each of the steps is usually in operation all through the process. Nevertheless, the reader will be able to note each particular step as it is being emphasized in the account which follows.

Clarifying the Problem

The Problem: HOW CAN WE MAKE OUR NEIGHBORHOOD A BETTER PLACE IN WHICH TO LIVE?

A. *The problem was approached by asking each child to write on the following topics:*
   1. The things I like best in our neighborhood
   2. The things I like least in our neighborhood
   3. The things I like best about the people in our neighborhood
   4. The things I like least about the people in our neighborhood

B. *The results were tabulated by the teacher, and listed on the board. As a result of the discussion with the children, they raised these questions:*
   1. How can we make our neighborhood a better place in which to live?
   2. How can we get a playground?
   3. How can we get people to do the right thing?
   4. How can we get people to understand the needs of children?
   5. What are the responsibilities of children in our neighborhood?

C. *Selection of major problems for class:*
   1. Many of the items listed by children dealt with recreation.
      a. We re-examined the lists which had been made by the class, and listed all the items dealing with recreation.

b. After further discussion, we decided that the problem, "How can we make our neighborhood a better place in which to live?" was worthwhile, but too broad in scope.

c. The problem, "How can we get a playground?" was the one most of the class wanted answered, but it was too limited. We enlarged it to, "How can we get more of what we need for recreation?"

d. We again examined the problems in the light of these questions which were asked by the teacher:

   (1) With which can we do the most?
   (2) From which will we be able to get the best results?

e. The class decided that the problem dealing with recreation would be most profitable to them. So the subject for consideration was "How can we get more of what we need for recreation?" and, in particular, "How can we get a recreation center?"

f. Because the children felt that the other questions posed were of interest to them, we decided to clarify for our own benefit what we meant by them.

   (1) Teacher wrote these problems on board:
       (a) What do you mean by people doing the right thing?
       (b) What do you think are the needs of children?
       (c) What do you think are the responsibilities of children in a neighborhood?
   (2) We spent a short time discussing these questions.
   (3) Teacher listed children's suggestions on board.

g. Setting up criteria to determine if the major problem would be satisfactory to work with:

   (1) When we had decided the problem which we were going to consider, we set up standards by which we could judge the value of the problem. These are the criteria by which the class decided to judge it:
       (a) Will we benefit by it?

      (b) Is it important to us?

      (c) Will we be able to answer it?

      (d) Will we be able to do it intelligently?

      (e) Can it be worked out?

      (f) Can we get material to answer it?

      (g) Will it include the whole class?

  h. We tested the problem against each of these standards, and decided that we could answer "yes" to each of the questions.

Gathering . . . Organizing . . . Evaluating

A. *At the teacher's suggestion, the class decided that it had to list what it knew, and what it would have to know*

  1. What we know

    a. What recreation is

      (1) Defined by children as play, having fun, doing what you enjoy, relaxing, something to do for your own pleasure

    b. What kinds of things people do for recreation

  2. *What we have to know before we can find out what to do*

    a. What are the recreational facilities in our neighborhood?

    b. Can everyone use them?

    c. What do other people think would be good to have for recreation?

Other children	Principal
Parents	Neighbors

    d. What are the possibilities for recreation in our community?

      (1) Do we have space for recreation?

      (2) What kinds would we suggest?

      (3) Where would we put the facilities?

      (4) How large is our community?

      (5) How can we get the equipment we think we want?

   e. What does the City Planning Commission think
    desirable?
   f. What do other cities think?

B. *We decided we could get information from these sources:*
 1. People—we used children, principal, neighbors, parents, guests
 2. Books and pamphlets:
  a. *You and Your Neighborhood*—Stonorov and Kahn
  b. *Places for Playing in Cleveland*—Cleveland Planning Commission
  c. *Public Improvements, 1947-1952* — Philadelphia
   Planning Commission
 3. Pictures—children made scrapbooks
 4. Trips

C. *Before we could find out "How can we get more of what we
 want for recreation?" we thought we ought to know what
 our neighborhood is.*
 1. Each child thought the vicinity in which he lived was
  "our" neighborhood.
 2. We plotted on the board the streets where the children
  live.
 3. We discovered many individual neighborhoods over-
  lapped.
 4. All of them covered a large territory.
 5. We reached this decision:
  Our neighborhood consists of all the streets on which
  the children coming to the school live.
 6. Teacher asked—How can we get accurate information
  as to what streets send children to our school?
 7. After discussion, the class decided to ask the principal
  of the school.
 8. Discussion followed on how to approach the principal:
  a. By letter?
  b. By committee?
 9. Children decided on committee:
  a. Children chose committee of four children
  b. Decided what questions to ask

    c. Made an appointment to see principal

    d. Received map from principal with school boundaries outlined.

D. *We decided to make map of school neighborhood:*

  1. Map to include:

    a. Where we live

    b. Where we play

    c. Where we buy things

  2. Committee was chosen to make map.

E. *Each child made map of own street which included:*

  1. Houses   4. Lights

  2. Stores   5. Trolley tracks

  3. Lots

F. *To find out the recreational facilities in the neighborhood, the children listed the places where they play:*

  1. Street   6. Summer playground

  2. Houses   7. Backyard

  3. Schoolyard   8. Alleys

  4. Empty lots   9. Pavement

  5. Recreation center (small, in Hebrew School)

At this point one pupil, Charles, whose family had recently moved from the neighborhood, objected to planning because he no longer lived in the neighborhood. He did not feel he would benefit from such discussion.

The class in answering him, said:

  1. Everyone will benefit if we improve our neighborhood.

  2. People will be happy if our neighborhood is good; they won't be ashamed of it.

  3. If we don't fix our neighborhood, and no one else is interested, other neighborhoods will be bad, and it might even spread to Charles' neighborhood.

  4. Wasn't Charles glad when he moved out of this neighborhood? He was ashamed of it.

5. Almost all the parents would like to move. If we improved our neighborhood they would stay.
6. If we fix our neighborhood other people will take us as an example and fix theirs.
7. This isn't just for our benefit. It is for the city's benefit.
8. If children are safe, well, and happy in one neighborhood, everyone will benefit.
9. Play space will save lives.

G. *The children investigated the recreational facilities in the neighborhood. These were as follows:*
1. Schoolyard
2. Movies
3. Sunday school—summer activities
4. Small recreational center
5. Boys' Club (Crime Prevention Authority)

In discussion it developed that only white children were permitted to play at the recreation center. The children wanted to know why this was so, and decided to send a committee to find out.

They set up these standards for conducting an interview:

1. We must be very polite.
2. We must know what we are going to say.
3. We have to be very careful of the way we ask questions, so people won't get the wrong impression of us.
4. We have to be able to explain our problem.
5. We should express ourselves clearly.
6. We should listen carefully.
7. We must not argue.
8. We must try to convince other people of what we think, but we must do it tactfully.

Two boys were selected to interview the director of the recreation center. They made an appointment with him. When they reported the results, no one was satisfied with the response the boys had received. The man had refused to discuss the matter in any detail. He had said, "We wouldn't mind having them, but they fight all the time," and then had walked away. As a result of the discussion which followed, the class said:

1. It's wrong to keep Negro people out of the recreation center. It's not the color of a person that counts; it's the character.
2. The Negro children in our class are just as nice as any of the white children.
3. If they allow children of different religions to go there, they ought to allow Negro children. Keeping them out doesn't make sense.

The discussion went on to the question of discrimination in general society. One thing which bothered some of the white children is indicated in the following discussion:

"What if our parents won't let us play with Negro children? What can we do? They say we're too little and don't know anything."

"We're little and can't change our parents' minds. We can't do anything until we're old enough for them to listen to us. We can learn what is right now—keep on learning—and then act on it when we are older if our parents won't let us do it now."

"We mustn't change our minds about this as we grow older. We have to keep on learning. If we stop learning, we'll forget about it."

The teacher knew two of the white families who objected to their children associating with the Negro children. She decided to allow the class to express their opinions on the question.

H. *Planning a trip to see what was being done with recreation in other parts of city.*

1. With help of the Curriculum Office and the Philadelphia Housing Authority we planned for a trip to the

James Weldon Johnson Homes, and the Recreation Center at 11th and Huntington Streets.

2. Children set up standards for conduct:
   a. Behave
   b. Follow the leader
   c. Co-operate
   d. Don't touch anything
   e. Be quiet
   f. Have good manners
   g. Keep together

3. Children decided to take notes on trip so they would remember what they saw.

4. We decided we wanted to take the trip for the following reasons:
   a. Recreation center
      (1) Find out more about recreation.
      (2) Find out what kinds of recreation they have.
      (3) Get ideas of what we want.
      (4) See what they have that we do not have.
   b. Housing Project
      (1) Compare their houses with ours.
      (2) See how they arrange for play for children.

5. We planned to think about and look for these things on our trip:
   a. Empty lots
   b. Safe play places
   c. Streets and people
   d. Houses
   e. Gardens
   f. Street lights
   g. Transportation
   h. Parks
   i. Libraries
   j. Garbage disposal
   k. Shopping centers

I. *We took the trip:*

   1. Representatives of the Curriculum Office, and of the Philadelphia Housing Authority, accompanied us.

J. *On our return we:*

   1. Evaluated our behavior on basis of criteria set up
   2. Organized the facts gathered
   3. Wrote letters to thank those who helped us plan the trip

K. *Other class activities:*

1. Here, and at other points, we:
   a. Wrote stories about the trip and other phases of the work
   b. Wrote poems
   c. Sang songs
   d. Planned an issue of the class newspaper to deal with our problem
   e. Drew pictures
   f. Made scrapbooks
   g. Made bulletin boards

L. *We wanted to investigate our neighborhood:*

1. We divided the area into sections.
2. Children divided into committees, according to location of their homes.
3. We planned for each group to investigate its section and report on it.
4. We decided to look for

   a. Empty lots
   b. Gardens, trees, parks
   c. Houses
   d. Alleys
   e. Stores
   f. Condition of streets
   g. Transportation
   h. Traffic lights
   i. Play spaces
   j. Synagogues and churches

5. We planned to take one neighborhood walk with the whole class:

   a. We made a map of the area we planned to explore.
   b. We planned particular route to follow.
   c. We made arrangements to visit Boys Club on walk.
      (1) Committee went to director of club to make arrangements.
      (2) Sent letter to director to confirm appointment.

6. We took the trip, making notes on the way.
7. Committees took trips to other sections as planned.
8. Committee reported findings.

M. *We gathered all the facts we had found.*

At this point on basis of evidence, the class decided there was no place big enough in the neighborhood for a recreation center. The class agreed that they needed expert advice. We sent letters inviting representatives of the Curriculum Office and the Philadelphia Housing Authority to come to our class to help us.

N. *A collaborator in Open-mindedness Study visited the class.*

The teacher had acquainted the collaborator with the situation. The class was unaware of this fact, and did not know that he was there for a particular reason. They were very curious when he wrote on the board, without comment, "We are stuck! We need help! We are in a jam!" The discussion which followed, showed a rather interesting experience in critical analysis. These are exact quotations from the children's responses.

"What is our trouble? What is wrong? What is bothering us? We have to find out."

"I think we are in trouble. We haven't asked our parents to co-operate yet."

"We don't want to ask for help unless we know what we want."

"Let's look back at our work and see if our trouble is in our back work, or something we are coming to."

"Have we made a mistake, or are we coming to our trouble now? If we're coming to it, maybe it will be easier to change beforehand."

"We have looked for places where we could put a recreation center or a playground. We saw only small lots. We can't have a recreation center with what we saw. No space was big enough."

"That's why we're stuck. Because we haven't a big empty space to use."

The collaborator asked what they were going to do. They said they had asked for help.

> One child said, "The Railway Express Yard would be a wonderful place if we could get it. Let's find out if we could have that for a play space."

> "It would be silly to ask for that space. They are making a living there. My father wouldn't give up his store even if a playground is needed. My mother is very much interested in our problem. She would contribute money. But interested as she is, I think she'd kick me out if I asked her for the store. It's more important to eat and sleep than it is to play."

The collaborator told them he would like to know their decision after they had spoken to the people they had invited.

   O. *In response to the children's invitations a representative of the Curriculum Office and of the Philadelphia Housing Authority came to the class on two different days.*

   1. The visit of the representative of the Curriculum Office.
       a. Some of the discussion went as follows:
           (1) "We're up against a stone wall. We took walks in our neighborhood, and didn't find any place big enough to build a recreation center."
           (2) "We have another problem. Children live on both sides of Girard Avenue. It's dangerous to cross the street. We have to think about where children live before we decide on a place."
           (3) "We'll be lucky to get any play space anywhere. If we can get something near school, we ought to take it. We have to start somewhere."

The discussion went on to a comparison of the Housing Project we visited and the school neighborhood. It also involved the housing situation in the neighborhood. The children decided that groups of people working together could get more done than individuals working alone.

At the conclusion of the visit, however, they had not yet resolved their problem.

2. The visit of the representative of the Philadelphia Housing Authority.
   a. The representative asked, "What is your problem?"
   b. Children: "We can't find a place big enough for play space."
   c. Discussion followed on:
      (1) How much space do we need?
      (2) How much space do we have?
      (3) Who is going to use the space?
   d. As a result of this discussion, the children changed their original plan of trying to get a recreation center.
   e. The time element was also discussed. The end of the term was approaching and there was a possibility the problem could not be completed.

DECISION

A. *Since we can't get a large space for a recreation center, we'll try to get several small lots in different parts of the neighborhood which we can fix up and use to play on.*

B. *We decided that if we couldn't finish we would go as far as possible, because the problem is worth while.*

ACTION TAKEN

A. *Children measured the size of neighborhood lots on a land-use map.*

B. *The children decided they would plan to equip play lots so that children from nine to twelve years old could play on them.*

C. *They decided they would have lots for different purposes:*
   1. Baseball
   2. General play

3. Discussed what games they could play:
   a. Box ball
   b. Swings
   c. Sliding board
   d. Checkers and dominoes
   e. Jumping rope
   f. Hop-scotch
   g. Baseball
   h. Soft ball
   i. Hand ball

4. Discussed what would have to be done to lots before they could be used.

5. Invited parents to class to discuss problem.
   a. Wrote letters asking parents to come
   b. Presented problem to parents (a majority of parents were present)
      (1) Need for play space
      (2) Need of adult help
   c. Got from parents names of organizations to which they belonged on which they might call for help.
   d. Parents filled out questionnaires prepared by principal in connection with redevelopment program in which they stated what they wanted in neighborhood.

6. Committees of children chosen to measure lots in neighborhood.

7. Made board maps of lots according to scale.

8. Plotted on board where equipment could be put on lots.

9. Discussed which lots would be most desirable from the standpoint of—
   a. Space
   b. The number of children who lived closest to them

10. Found names of owners of lots.
    a. Teacher got information from City Hall.

11. Wrote letters to owners of lots explaining:
    a. Why we wanted lots
    b. Asking for appointment with owners to meet them

12. Interviewed neighbors to see how they would feel about our using lots for play space.
    a. In class, discussed approach to neighbors. We set up a situation in class, with some children acting as neighbors, others as members of class.

13. Neighbors reactions favorable to idea.

14. Discussed results of answers to our letters.
    a. One owner offered use of lots.
        (1) Another lot we hoped to use adjoins the lot which was offered, but by the end of the term we had not heard from the second owner.
        (2) Several people we had written to said we didn't own the lots. Teacher said she would have to get further information from City Hall, tracing the titles to the lots.

15. When we reached this phase of the work, the term ended.
    a. Teacher and class had discussion.
        (1) Teacher said, "We can't go on with our work now; what shall we do?"
        (2) Class decided they would like to think ahead.
        (3) Some possibilities for future
            (a) Try to get new teachers to carry on the project.
            (b) If not, work with present teacher after school.
            (c) Think of where we will get money.
            (d) Get other children in school interested.

SUMMARY OF CHILDREN'S REACTIONS TO WORK DONE

At the end of the term we recapitulated the work we had done, and on the basis of our findings, we came to the following decisions. These are in the teacher's words.

1. We evaluated the process we were using in solving our problems, and decided it was an efficient way to work.
2. We evaluated the problem and decided it was worthwhile.
3. We realized that community improvement is a long range program.
4. We realized that group action is important in solving community problems.
5. We realized that the individual has a share and responsibility in improving the community.
6. We concluded that a complete solution of a community problem is not always possible at the time.

7. We realized that the solution of our problem might not be achieved immediately because it is part of a complex situation.

8. We realized that a large recreation center is not possible for us at the present time.

9. We decided it would be better for us to get small lots in various areas of the neighborhood to be used for play space.

10. We concluded that we would have to keep on working on the problem if we hoped to achieve something concrete.

11. We thought that if people had been interested and constructively active many years ago, we would not have this pressing need now.

ACTIVITIES CARRIED ON THROUGHOUT ENTIRE PERIOD OF TIME DEVOTED TO PROBLEM

1. *We used maps:*
   a. We made maps to scale
   b. We made maps of the neighborhood
   c. We made maps planning trips
   d. We made maps of lots
   e. We used a land-use map
   f. We enlarged spaces according to scale
   g. We read and interpreted maps
2. *We estimated sizes of lots*
3. *We measured lots*
4. *We compared sizes of lots*
5. *We made plans for use of lots*
6. *Language:*
   a. We wrote letters
   b. We wrote stories
   c. We wrote poems
   d. We wrote a class newspaper
   e. We used new spelling words involved in problem
   f. We defined new words and terms used
   g. Reading
      Pamphlets and books

7. *Music:*
   Songs about recreation, from books and original ones

8. *Art:*
   a. Pictures drawn by children
   b. Pictures from magazines
   c. Bulletin board displays
   d. Scrapbooks

9. *We made extensive use of discussion techniques*
10. *We took trips.*

PERSPECTIVE

One of the most difficult phases in any project is that of getting off to a good start. "Well begun is half done" is an old adage that applies as much to beginning a school-community activity as it does to a task which the individual sets for himself. The reports presented here make clear that no blueprint exists for the initiation of community-school co-operation—neither for who begins it, nor for how the initial steps should be taken. The activities reported were inaugurated by different people—by teachers, by children, by interested citizens and by professors.

The rural program developed when a tenant farmer recognized his problem, and fortunately for him knew where to turn for help. For the school personnel to be hospitable to lay people who need help seems an important aspect of all community schools. To develop a warm, welcoming school atmosphere wherein the confidence and respect of community people can flourish is an essential achievement. It was not necessary in Pilot Point for the farmer to search for books on his problem or even to write to a distant state college for help. The hospitable climate was there and the local teacher already had the "know-how." He was not only able to give advice desired, but was able to assist its operation. Both of these factors have significant implications for teacher education. If community participation by teachers in rural areas is to be effective, they must learn many more skills than the average teacher now develops in the usual teacher-education program; even in those of the best teachers colleges and university schools of education.

The town project was begun by children with a social problem, present and pressing for answers. A problem is an excellent place to begin learning as well as a good place to begin teaching. In any study of activities which involve the community the problem approach seems desirable, especially in the process of getting started. However, the acceptance of problems suggested by children is one which requires the wisest discrimination by teachers. Too frequently there is but a vague differentiation between the problems of actual concern to adults and the problems of actual concern to the learners. It is all to the good, apparently, when the problem has both characteristics—as it did in the high-cost-of-living study. This is a matter of community concern but has personal implication, even for twelve-year-olds.

The small city report is a good illustration of how university professors and their students used the community in an effort to understand its problems through firsthand experiences. Teachers of professional subjects in the colleges who educate teachers can learn much from these reports. Too often educational sociology is taught almost wholly through vicarious experiences—by the use of textbooks and films. This is an easy way to teach, but the behavior of many teachers in local communities casts serious doubt on whether or not learning takes place during the teaching. For adults, as with children, there seems to be no substitute for direct experiences. Interviews, surveys, field trips, service projects and work experiences have a vivid learning quality which cannot be ignored in teaching, though many college professors succeed very well in so doing. Unfortunately for those who cling only to textbooks, social motivation is rarely the result of intellectual comprehension. It is nearly always the result of emotional conditioning. People must feel strongly about problems before they make serious efforts to solve them, and feelings are more likely than not to develop from experiences.

Good practices emerge from these reports and they suggest methods with wide applications. In general, the people developing the community projects here reported not only began with a real problem right at hand, they used also the resources available to attack it. This practice held true for all of the reports examined for possible inclusion in Part II of this book, and is specifically apparent in the four cases chosen for presentation in the present chapter. In the report of the rural school for example, the agricultural teacher and his class moved out of the classroom into the fields of the tenant farmer where demonstration and participation on the part of the teachers and students began the project. Practical demonstration with natural resources has high value in teaching at any point, but at the beginning of a project it seems invaluable. Direct participation of the students followed the demonstrations. This practice, too, is valuable as everyone knows who has worked with young learners. In most schools, especially if they are small and rural, opportunities are ever present to make education more functional and life-like. The trouble is that many rural teachers are unaware of the vital community needs which surround them, and if by chance such needs are called to their attention they do not know how to proceed to meet them.

The report of the small town illustrates also the use of resources. There the teacher wisely used the materials close at hand and available to most children—the daily newspaper, radio broadcasts, conferences with parents and so on. Likewise, in the small city report such resources as political parties, governmental agencies, and social welfare groups were used with good effect. The Metropolitan report with its emphasis on local recreation underscores the point. Apparently, the extension of the curriculum by bringing the local problems into the school is likely to be stymied in the beginning if resources are not available to stimulate interest and keep it going.

Another practice of promise was the evidence of lead-on projects—outgrowths of the solutions for original problems. These hold great promise to be sure but they also present problems. One of the difficult problems in the organization of learning experiences is to know when to follow a new interest of the children, when it is only slightly related to the old. A good illustration of how to take this hurdle successfully is found in the report from the small town school, in the instance of the allied project of CARE. Not only was this interest made a learning experience in itself, but important values inherent in a democracy were emphasized. These, as in many outcomes of lead-on projects, may be more significant for children than the values inherent in the original problem.

Thirdly, in all the reports there is evidence of the use of organized groups who worked as teams on local problems. This is a good teaching procedure, perfectly at home in acceptable democratic practices. The teacher and children in the metropolitan report well illustrate this practice. Here the children used the committee technique in that strategic phase of the project when it was necessary to gather and organize facts. It was at this point, too, when children moved into the community. Committees of children going into the community to secure needed facts seem a more sensible procedure than for individuals to do so.

Moreover, children attacking community problems together learn from one another. They assist one another in setting up criteria, in gathering facts, and in how to act professionally as they seek them.

A fourth practice of promise was the emphasis placed in the community projects on the generalization of experiences. Frequently exponents of firsthand experiences in learning assume that having an experience is an end in itself. This concept, however, is contrary to the facts. Education is more than feeling and reactions to experience. An experience is learning but it becomes education only as it is subjected to interpretation and evaluation. Moreover, it must somehow be linked with larger aspects of a problem. In other words, the learner must be assisted in generalizing his experiences. While the activities of the learner were emphasized in these reports, their discussions with the generalizations which followed seem particularly desirable. Frequently, insufficient attention is given to helping children think about and understand the activities in which they are engaged. It is possible for a group to spend a great deal of time going about the community gathering facts, trying to persuade people to paint their houses and control flies, and do so without actually learning very much. Helping a community secure adequate recreational facilities is a worthwhile activity but it is much more valuable when accompanied by efforts to think about and generalize on the experience. There is, happily, considerable evidence in these reports that efforts were made to "intellectualize" the community experiences, and this is important. Seeing that learners get some large ideas from their experiences is a fundamental obligation of the school.

Finally, in all of these reports it is evident that the people who began the school community projects had a special point-of-view about education. All of them believed that education is a process which extends outward from the school to the community, and also inward from the community to the school. These people also believed that all citizens are responsible in a direct way for the education of the youth in a community, and that the responsibility should be recognized and assumed. Moreover, the originators of the school-community activities here reported are convinced that education has a direct responsibility for the improvement of the quality of living of the community which supports the school. The beliefs and values which people hold about education are basic in the development of the school within the community. Indeed, these seem to precede action and should have precedence over it.

4
Going Forward

It is one thing to begin school-community activities, and another to move ahead successfully with them. Many teachers and many schools have begun community projects in high hopes, only to abandon them before they were well begun. As pointed out in the section *Getting Started,* the persistence of community school activities, as well as the process of getting them started, requires a fundamental educational point of view. Unless the teacher or group of teachers, and the administrators or the school as a whole, has the community concept of the educational process, the so-called community school activities are likely to be transitory, over-dramatized, and of little real significance. It is one thing to give lip-service to the community concept in education, and quite another to give it the support of the long pull in moving forward. Too many so-called community schools have made auspicious beginnings, only to lose momentum and drop by the wayside for various reasons—when a vigorous leader left, or there was continued bad weather which interfered with regular meetings, or "the people just lost interest." Yet difficulties are usually more deep-seated than these reasons would suggest, and often can be found in the second stage of the establishment of good community-school relations.

Many community schools are begun with all the enthusiasms characteristic of first discoveries. Often educational leaders sincerely believe that they have made discoveries, unique in education. As a matter of fact, the community-school concept is centuries old. It belongs to no one person, to no single age.[1]

Although the concept is old, the methods of moving the idea forward and getting it into sustained operation are still new to most school people. Techniques are many and varied as the following several accounts of successful practice can merely suggest.

GREENHOW SCHOOL
SPREADS ITS WINGS [2]

This is the story of a small rural school . . . and it has a real moral for those who look for such implications. It tells how one school influenced a whole county. It illustrates the principle that education is a process of improving people and of helping them to live better in the school, the home, and the community. It is a good story—good because it reports a sustained program of sound educational action.

The Greenhow community lies in the northern part of Florida, in a section much like Georgia. The climate is mild, and the land rich and productive. Sea Island cotton, tobacco, peanuts and sweet potatoes grow there in abundance. The community is located in the same county, Leon County, in which is found the capital of the state.

To appreciate this account one must understand how the

[1] See Joseph K. Hart, *A Social Interpretation of Education* (New York: Henry Holt, 1929).

[2] Reported by Mrs. Dorothy G. Holmes, "Jeanes Teacher," Leon County, Florida.

agricultural agent and the Jeanes teacher [3] work together in Leon County. These two leaders know that if the lot of rural people is to be improved it will be done through the improvement of land and the improvement of people. Moreover, they recognize the important part played by the schools in these two related processes. The agricultural agent and the Jeanes teacher had seen the Greenhow people's interest in improving crops and children. Both leaders believed that by helping the people to help themselves a truly functional community school might be developed to benefit the Negro people of the community.

A meeting on strategy was called, and to it came, besides the two leaders named above, the Home Demonstration Agent, the School Lunch Supervisor, the County Nurse, the vocational agricultural teacher from the nearest high school, a representative from the Florida A & M College, and the Superintendent of Public Instruction. At the meeting a community council was organized, with the Jeanes teacher as co-ordinator. A community and a school survey were planned.

When the surveys were completed, the facts discovered provided the clues to needed improvements. Homes were found to be crowded, dilapidated, and lacking in sanitary facilities. Malnutrition, malaria, and hookworm were prevalent among the people. In spite of the rich soil and lush climate, the average cash revenue per farm family was found to be only $300 per year. The school had no water on the grounds, no electricity, and no lunch room. The school grounds were unattractive, neglected.

A faculty meeting of the Greenhow School was called and the facts presented. The group decided to stress the

[3] In the South the Negro Supervisor of Rural Schools is frequently called "the Jeanes Teacher" because this county office was originally made possible through the philanthropy of Miss Anna T. Jeanes.

community's better housing, and to do this through the curriculum materials of the school. Tentative plans were made.

The children in the first, second, and third grades worked on a doll house, which they planned and built. Pupils in the middle grades concentrated their efforts on the school garden, and on the yard. The oldest children in the upper grades specialized on the reconditioning of furniture.

The results of the work of the children on their several projects were satisfactory if not spectacular. Enough vegetables were grown to help considerably with the lunch program, shrubbery was planted, and a concrete walk laid down. The children learned how to recondition old furniture "to look better than the new." They learned to make hampers for soiled clothes, kitchen curtains, and table napkins. They also learned about setting tables properly, and that eating is a ceremony with rules. The enthusiasm of the children for the improvement of their school-home was contagious—soon parents caught it, too. They supplemented the money donated by the Board for a school piano, for a new pump, and for the concrete walk. With the further assistance of the adults, rural electrification was brought into the community and made available to the school. The school building was reconditioned and a kitchen added.

Student teachers from the Agricultural Department of the nearby A & M College worked three days a week with the older boys and with the community adults. Together they constructed a flag pole, repaired and painted the fence, built flower boxes and magazine racks. Farmers and the older boys were assisted with butchering hogs and grinding the sugar cane. Feed hoppers, water troughs, and hen nests were built.

The teachers in the school opened the school building on certain nights a week for a well-planned recreational program—parties, fish-fries, community sings, group games, and movies. Club work was begun with the children and three groups were organized at the school—Boy Scouts, New Homemakers of America, and the Boys Social Club. All became active in this on-going community program.

Two important projects were undertaken by the Home Makers Club. The new lunch room was made attractive by new cabinets, painted walls, linoleum for the floor, and attractive window curtains. The girls in the Club also made luncheon sets, rugs, bed spreads, belts, hats, and other articles useful at home.

The Boys Club members specialized on the school playground. With money they earned they purchased two basketballs, one volley ball and net, a baseball and bat, and several indoor games.

The Boy Scout Troop was the first rural troop organized in a rural school in Leon County. Sponsored by the PTA, the troop was soon busy with plans for useful contributions to the community, especially in helping secure the playground equipment for the school.

The local Health Department co-operated in providing physical examinations, including blood tests, for every child in school. Many physical defects were thus discovered among the children, and plans were made for their early correction.

From this co-operative effort of professional agencies, school children, and community adults the following beneficent results can be enumerated:

1. The Board of Public Instruction has been alerted to the needs of all of the Negro schools of the county. Since the project in Greenhow was begun, ten small schools for Negroes have been abandoned and five school buses provided to transport the children to larger and better schools.
2. Adults have improved their own homes.

3. Children have learned to improve their homes through the use of free and inexpensive materials.
4. Children have learned the importance of good health, of having safe water and sanitary toilets at home and at school.
5. Through the school-lunch program the children have learned to prepare well-balanced meals, have learned to eat many foods that they were not accustomed to eating, and have learned good table manners by practicing them every day.
6. Through the work of such clubs as the Boy Scouts and the New Home Makers of America, desirable qualities of citizenship have been developed.
7. All agencies in the community are working co-operatively with the school to help raise the social and economic level of the people.
8. The school enrollment has increased, so that Greenhow now has four teachers. The great need at present is for additional classrooms.

DEVELOPING A COMMUNITY RESOURCES FILE [4]

The use of local resources in teaching is perhaps the oldest and certainly one of the most commonly used ways to interest both teachers and lay people in community education. This report indicates in some detail how educators and lay citizens worked together to survey the educational resources of their community as a basis for developing a community resources information file. While the file itself is very important, the side values of better school-community relations may have even greater significance, as this account suggests.

[4] Reported by Arthur E. Hamalainen, Chairman of the Curriculum Coordinating Committee, Manhasset Public Schools, Manhasset, New York.

The teachers in the public schools of Manhasset, New York, like those in all modern schools, have used community resources in many ways. At various times field trips have been taken to places of educational interest, pupils have participated in community enterprises, and members of the community have come to the school or have been visited by children to discuss topics ranging from animals to world affairs.

In spite of the frequent use of community resources thus made there have been many occasions when teachers discovered resources that might have been advantageously used in an area already covered. Some of these teachers began to ask, "Why not develop an information file where a teacher can go to see what resources are available in the community before the actual teaching of any unit is begun?" This question soon was discussed at length by the Curriculum Co-ordinating Committee. The final decision was to build such a file for each school. During these first discussions it was brought out that here was an excellent chance to get interested community members working with the Committee, since it would be a project in which lay people could readily see their own contribution. Members from both the School Community Association (a group of lay people interested in the public schools) and members of the largest civic association volunteered their services after the plan was explained to them.

Some of the problems which arose were these:

1. Should a complete community survey be made in order that all important human and material resources be covered?
2. If a complete community survey were made, what method would be used to discover these resources?
3. What areas should be included in a community resources file for Manhasset?
4. On what basis should individual and material resources be selected for inclusion in the file?

5. What method of classification should be used in compiling the file?
6. Should human and material resources be listed in the same file?
7. Should this file be made available to the general community as well as to the schools?

As the work of the committee progressed, it was decided not to make a complete community survey but to gather information about field trip opportunities, possible resource people, and teaching materials such as booklets, photographs, collections, and the like. Three procedures were followed:

1. Each lay person on the committee contacted various organizations in the community to find out what materials and resources might be available from within these groups. The lay people also obtained suggestions from these organizations concerning other sources.
2. The lay people were asked to uncover through their own personal contacts any sources they knew might be available for the file.
3. All the teachers in the Manhasset schools were asked to survey the cumulative records of each child and to list parents who might be classified in the index.

The information gathered in this manner was brought to the committee meetings and evaluated for the file, and the various purposes for which the data might be used were discussed. At the end of the year, this information was listed on file cards. These cards were developed by the group itself from suggestions made by many teachers.

In order that the file might not become encumbered with material of little or no value, the permanent standing committee (composed of lay people and teachers) meets four times each year to go through the index and refine it. This committee, furthermore, gathers other material such as booklets, pamphlets, models, etc., which are available to all teachers.

This project met with enthusiastic approval by both the teachers group and the entire community. From it grew more active participation of the lay people on the Curriculum Co-ordinating Committee. At the present time there are about twenty-five parents working with various committees on educational problems confronting the Manhasset School System.

The response of the teachers and lay people to the community resources file led to the formulation of a questionnaire, submitted to all teachers and interested lay persons, which asked them to list the most important problems which they felt existed in the schools. The problems listed by these people furnished the basis of work for these lay-teacher committees. Among the problems currently receiving this school-community attention are these:

1. Using community resources effectively
2. Newer approaches to the learning process
3. Utilizing audio-visual resources to best advantage
4. Helping children who have problems

As the above procedures are continued, it is planned to extend the curriculum work to even more members of the community, and to make the school more truly life-centered in their approach to helping children.

COMMUNITY LOOKS
AT ITS SCHOOLS [5]

*Let us take a look at our schools. It really seems to be
a sensible thing to do in view of the heavy investment
the community has in education. Add to that the fact
that the schools have been running pretty much on
their own for as long as the oldest citizen can recall.
Is it not time to take an inventory of a community institution that means so much in the lives of all of us,
rich and poor, young and old, teachers and parents,
students and graduates? The people of Urbana, Illinois, said, "Yes," and this is their story.*

Urbana is a typical midwestern city, distinguished prin-
cipally as the county seat of Champaign County and the
home of the University of Illinois. Its population has grown
steadily and now numbers more than 23,000 people. Urbana has never become industrialized to any great extent,
since the city of Champaign just to the west has tended to
absorb most of the industrial enterprises in the community.
It does, however, provide merchandising outlets for agricultural products. The present school system includes one four-
year high school, one two-year junior high school, six
elementary schools housing grades one to six inclusive, and
one primary center that has pupils in grades one, two and
three only. The total enrollment is more than 2,300. Approximately 1,400 children are in the first six grades, and
the others are in the upper six grades.

[5] Reported by C. C. Loew and M. R. Sumption in the *Nation's Schools*
46:40-43; December, 1950.

Early in the school year of 1948 the board of education gave voice to what had been in the minds of many teachers and other members of the community when it said, "Let's take a look at our schools."

Perhaps the most urgent problem was the fact that the school population was fast outgrowing the housing facilities, and the board members and the new superintendent fully realized that the situation was becoming acute.

In the second place, although the educational program probably was no better and no worse than that of most cities the size of Urbana, the question arose as to whether it could be made better. Some questions frequently asked were, "Is our educational program meeting the real needs of the community?" "Is there need for expansion in areas such as preschool, adult, vocational and consumer education?" Are we shortchanging the exceptional child?" "Is our school organization efficient?" "Can we afford the kind of educational program we think desirable?"

It was from this situation that the idea of a co-operative survey grew. The board and the superintendent recognized that within the professional staff and the local community there existed many competencies that would prove invaluable in any appraisal. It also was recognized that professional consultation should supplement the work of the community and that the staff members of the University of Illinois College of Education could give guidance where needed.

Therefore in September, when the co-operation of the university was assured, the project was inaugurated. It was launched with the clear understanding that it was to be a community project, although the field-service staff of the college of education would set up a survey structure, suggest methods and technics for study, and provide guidance and advice as it was needed. The responsibility for carrying the project through to completion rested squarely upon the members of the local school staff and upon the other citizens of the community. The plan of the survey was based upon the theory that if teachers, students and other citizens of the community studied the problem at firsthand they not only would see the needs and help formulate a program to meet them, but also would give full support to a sound educational blueprint for their community.

Three Committees Chosen

The first job of the board of education, on which it spent several weeks, was that of the selection of a citizens central committee for the survey. Every attempt was made to select representative citizens of proved ability who would be willing to give time and effort to the project. Twelve citizens were invited, in a letter which explained the plan and purpose of the study, to become members of this central committee. Each of the eleven who agreed to serve on this committee accepted the responsibility and gave whole-hearted support to the project. Members of a second central committee of thirteen teachers were selected by the teaching staff itself. The nine student members of a third central committee were selected by the student body.

Interlocking Committees, Too

Each of these central committees assumed primary responsibility for one or more areas of the study. Each formed subcommittees enlisting additional citizens, teachers and students in the various phases of the enterprise. The chairmanship of these subcommittees was sometimes assumed by a member of the central committee, but in many cases subcommittees operated without central committee personnel. These subcommittees made extensive studies of specific phases of the educational program assigned to them by the central committees and brought back reports.

The various members of the three central committees worked in close relationship and served on a number of interlocking committees that helped to co-ordinate the work of the survey. For example, a building committee, composed of laymen, teachers and students, accompanied by a member of the university staff, made a careful inspection of the school buildings. The members of this interlocking committee were then able to report back to their respective central committees on the condition of the school buildings in the system.

At the first meeting of the central committees each one selected its chairman and secretary. With the help of university staff members, the structure of the survey was decided upon and areas of specialization for each committee were selected. For example, the students' committee undertook as its special assignment the responsibility for collecting all pertinent facts about the community, its resources, population and vocational opportunities. This committee not only enlisted the aid of many students but also drew heavily on laymen in the community for necessary data. Several members of the citizens central committee made important contributions to the students' report.

In the areas of curriculum and staff personnel the teaching staff assumed leadership but made wide use of laymen in their analyses and appraisals.

Buildings, finance and general administration were the primary responsibility of laymen, who worked closely with local teachers and administrators and members of the university staff.

Phases of Survey

The first phase of the study necessarily consisted of obtaining and interpreting facts. This was an activity in which all committees and subcommittees shared. The information obtained was submitted by subcommittees to the central committees, which then shared the collected data by means of mimeographed reports and central committee meetings at which representatives of other committees gave oral reports. Furthermore, the chairmen of the three committees kept in close working relationship and acted as a co-ordinating force to ensure that each committee was kept up to date on the progress of the survey.

The second phase of the study involved a careful appraisal and analysis of the facts obtained and of their implications for improving the educational program of the community. The survey committees frankly faced facts and did not spare themselves or the schools in pointing out weaknesses and inadequacies. Good things were found, too, and they were brought to the attention of all committee members.

The study, however, was primarily oriented toward finding out wherein the educational program was failing to meet the needs of the people. For example, the guidance program was critically appraised in the light of the facts obtained about the pupil population, the drop-out rate, vocational opportunities in the community, and general community resources. Citizens committee members who were business executives examined the administrative setup with an eye to discovering inefficiencies and inadequacies. Their appraisal was submitted to the central committees so that the reactions of teachers, administrators, and students could be determined. These reactions served to modify, in some respects, the appraisal given by laymen. A glance at pupil population trends and the report of the housing subcommittee convinced everyone that new school buildings were needed. The study of the financial condition of the district served to convince even the most conservative members of the committees that the community could well afford to support an expanded curriculum and a school building program.

The third phase of the study consisted of the formulation and co-ordination of a series of recommendations. These recommendations were based on the pertinent facts that had been unearthed, the analysis and evaluation of these facts, and the desire to obtain for the community the best educational program it could afford.

The process by which these recommendations were arrived at was quite simple. Each subcommittee submitted recommendations for the area to which it was assigned. These recommendations were then carefully considered by the appropriate central committee. In some cases they were modified or changed to avoid duplication and to effect unity. In cases of disagreement the chairman of the subcommittee in question was called in, and the matter was discussed. However, the central committees assumed responsibility for the tentative recommendations in the areas assigned to them.

When the tentative recommendations in all areas had been completed, they were mimeographed and submitted to all members of the three central committees. Then followed a series of individual and joint central committee meetings out of which grew the final recommendations that were adopted by the central committees and incorporated into the final report. Specific recommendations for the improvement of the school program were made in the following areas: student personnel, staff personnel, elementary education, secondary education, services for exceptional children, co-curricular activities, administration, the school plant, and financing the schools.

During the course of the survey, wide publicity was given to it by newspapers, radio stations, and other mediums of communication. This publicity dealt with the methods and technics of the study, the personnel involved, and the facts discovered, but not with the recommendations. Publicity on the recommendations of the survey came after the final report had been submitted to the board of education and considered by the Board.

The work of compiling the report and producing more than 300 copies was jointly shared by the central committees and the College of Education staff.

Ten months after the survey began, the chairman of the citizens central committee made the formal presentation of the survey report to the board of education. The president of the board, in accepting the report, expressed his gratitude for the time and effort spent in constructive work by all those participating in the survey. He further promised that the board of education would give the report most careful study and take action at the earliest possible moment.

What Urbana Did

When school opened the following autumn, just one year after the survey was inaugurated, the board of education had given general endorsement to the recommendations of the survey, and the implementation of the survey program began. First of all, in a week-long planning conference, the teachers and the administrators laid plans for putting the survey recommendations into effect. They realized they were launching a long-range program, but they were eager to begin and were confident that great strides could be made that year.

Four implementation groups were set up to work with the board of education in carrying out the recommendations of the survey. These four groups were organized around the following areas: philosophy, curriculum, guidance and public relations. The specific purpose of these professional groups was to co-operate with the board of education in actually seeing that the recommendations were carried out. They were determined that the planning and working together during the last year should bear fruit. They were convinced that only by consistent co-operative effort could the goals set up in the survey be attained.

With a few exceptions, teachers and administrators accepted membership in the groups. The general feeling was that they shared in a task that promised rich rewards for themselves and their community. The work of these groups was directed toward making desirable changes as quickly as possible, both in their own right and through the board of education.

The group working in the area of philosophy set itself the task of translating the philosophy and objectives of the school, as expressed in the survey report, into attitudes, understandings, skills and concepts which, in turn, could be used by the classroom teacher in her daily work. It tried to help teachers improve their classroom practices in an attempt to make these more consistent with the expressed philosophy of the schools.

The group working with the implementation of curriculum recommendations considered reading basic to curriculum improvement, since it is the common denominator of the whole program, and made the concentrated study of this problem one of its first projects. In approaching the problem of dealing with children as individuals in reading, as well as in other areas, this group is offering additional evidence to the board of the need for more school space and smaller classes, both of which were recommended in the survey report. The group plans to continue the work of analyzing each subject-matter field in the light of its contribution to the needs of students and to recommend continued revision in line with changing needs. Ways and means were devised to expand offerings, in the light of discovered needs, as rapidly as facilities and staff could be provided.

In order to facilitate its work, members of this group requested that the College of Education set up a course in curriculum development specifically designed to help them achieve their goals. This was done in the spring.

The group devoting itself to guidance immediately began trying to formulate a better reporting system so that both parents and students might have a more meaningful appraisal of school work. This was in line with the recommendation of the survey, which called for a complete overhauling of the marking and reporting system. A second task was the revision of the student-record system, and the third was the establishment of a closer relationship between the guidance program and the resources of the community. The need for work on both these problems had been stressed in the survey report.

The group concerned with publicity adopted as one of its purposes the expansion of the public relations program of the Urbana schools by making teachers more aware of their responsibilities and by acquainting the public with the actual classroom work done in the schools. This group also offered its services to the board in connection with the new school building program.

For its part the board of education, in line with recommendations of the survey, employed architects and began the urgent job of getting the recommended building program under way. As preliminary drawings were made, the board sought advice from various committee members. The building program was discussed at parent-teacher meetings, and the location of the site of the proposed Southeast School was discussed at an open meeting. The board members felt that the whole project was a community enterprise and treated it as such. The survey committees and the board of education received gratifying evidence of the community's support for their work in a bond election in which the voters overwhelmingly approved a school building bond issue of more than $1,500,000.

From time to time the professional groups at work in the four areas mentioned make reports to the board of education, while the board in turn makes known to the staff its progress. The survey report, which is available to all teachers and members of the community, is serving as a flexible blueprint to point the way to a better school program for Urbana.

THE JORDAN
COMMUNITY CENTER [6]

Another way to move ahead in community school development is to organize a community council. The council is just what its name implies, and is composed usually of a representative group of citizens, organized to provide a medium for defining common community problems and planning their solution through

[6] Reported by the Director of the Council, Dorothy M. Chalgren.

*co-operative action. Initiative in forming a council
may come from a school or from some other community agency. This report tells how school-community
co-operation was started by the Council of Social
Agencies in Minneapolis, and how a junior high school
finally assumed responsibility for carrying it forward.*

In 1943 the Minneapolis Council of Social Agencies suggested that all communities in and around the city form
community councils for the purpose of studying local conditions and helping to solve neighborhood problems. A
control committee was set up to help the community work
get under way, and to serve as a clearing house for ideas
as well as a stimulating force in keeping community service
alive and functioning.

The Co-ordinating Committee now is composed of two
delegates from each council and two alternates, all elected
locally. A small budget is provided by the Council of Social
Agencies, which also furnishes a full-time secretary who
is an experienced social worker. The committee meets
monthly to hear reports of local councils, and to conduct
discussions of local problems. Once a year it conducts an
institute to stimulate interest. Seventeen community councils compose the organization in Hennepin County. Those
in suburban areas are too often "operating councils" that
actually organize and conduct social activities. Those in the
city are "co-ordinating councils" that serve to regulate,
stimulate, and co-ordinate the efforts of existing agencies.

The North Side Council was one of the first to be formed.
The officers were stimulated into action when the graduating class of Jordan Junior High School made a study of
the social and recreational opportunities offered children
and young people in that area. Data collected by the research department of the Council of Social Agencies was

studied by the students' committees, and the surveys were made by their classes.

Sense of Need

This study showed that citizens of North Minneapolis were not getting as much benefit from the fifty or more agencies of the Community Chest as were other sections of the city. For example, memberships in youth organizations, such as Boy and Girl Scouts, YMCA and YWCA groups were far below the city average. Local playgrounds, skating rinks, and park areas were more plentiful in South and West Minneapolis than they were on the North Side. The twenty schools of the city all had playgrounds but they were not open for use except during school time.

Three large social centers served restricted districts, one in a blighted semi-industrial area, one in the Negro section, and the third in a Jewish section. Four churches in this underprivileged area conducted part-time social and recreational programs.

All of these agencies were located in the older downtown section of North Minneapolis, but in the middle-class residential section surrounding the Jordan Junior High School there were no branch libraries, recreation centers, or adequate supervised playgrounds. Jordan Junior High School did have an extensive athletic program conducted by a branch of the YMCA, but during the depression the YMCA was charged a rental fee by the board of education for the use of its gymnasiums and swimming pools. This expense often restricted the service the YMCA could offer.

All of these and many other findings were presented to the North Side Community Council on Minneapolis statistical maps. Later, a youth council was formed from the civics classes of the four junior high schools on the North Side.

Youthful orators of all races and creeds made an impression on the adult leaders.

Minneapolis had a real handicap often found in cities which have grown rather rapidly: several boards or agencies supported by taxation were trying to conduct services in education, recreation, and welfare on a competitive basis without much attempt at co-ordination. The Board of Park Commissioners and the Library Board each had a generous budget for recreational and educational activities but each lacked facilities or space to carry on a program in some localities.

A new superintendent of schools, in 1944, immediately made a study of the $36,000,000 school plant and found practically all buildings closed during the late afternoon and evening hours. Yet the demand for opportunities for youth and adults to devote leisure time to recreational and educational activities was steadily increasing. More leisure time, which comes with technological advance and shorter working hours, unsettled national and international problems, growing juvenile delinquency and crime, higher costs of living, and the desire to advance through learning had a bearing upon this demand.

The following excerpt is taken from the Minneapolis School Report on Experimental Centers dated May 10, 1946:

> In consideration of these needs a number of committees from within and without the school system concurred in a recommendation that several community agencies co-operate in operating at least two experimental community centers in school buildings under the administration of the Minneapolis Public Schools. The following committees studied the problem, made preliminary surveys of community interest and need, developed community support and made recommendations:
>
>   Veterans' Educational Committee—Minneapolis Public
>   Schools

Wider Use of School Facilities Committee—Minneapolis
Public Schools

Public School Committee—Minneapolis Junior Association of Commerce

Co-ordinating Committee of Community Councils—Minneapolis Council of Social Agencies.

The administration of the Minneapolis Public Schools realized that school finances did not allow for the extensive development of community centers in schools. Furthermore, it was not possible to operate even two such community centers on an experimental basis without the co-operation of other community agencies in providing personnel and services to operate the program.

Community Committee

Administration officers of the following organizations and agencies agreed to participate in a co-operative venture and organized themselves into a co-ordinating committee for the City of Minneapolis:

Public Schools
Council of Parent-Teacher Association
Young Men's Christian Association
Board of Park Commissioners
Public Library
Junior Association of Commerce
Extension Division, University of Minnesota
Community Council's Co-ordinating Committee

The Co-ordinating Committee agreed on the following provisions:

1. That the community centers in schools will be administered by the Minneapolis Public Schools according to policies developed by the co-ordinating committee.

2. That each co-operating agency will contribute personnel and services in terms of its ability to do so, with authorization of its governing board.
3. That Bryant and Jordan Junior High Schools be the first experimental community centers.
4. That the experimental community centers be opened about October 1, 1946, and continue for approximately eight months.

Objectives of experimental community centers were established as follows:

1. To provide educational and recreational opportunities for youth and adults of the community adjacent to the community center.
2. To provide convenient meeting places, without charge, for organized and informal community groups.
3. To co-ordinate the services of several community agencies and organizations in one educational and recreational program.
4. To serve as a demonstration of the wider use of school facilities.
5. To experiment with indirect approaches to the problems of improving human relationships in the community.

Administration and financial arrangements were projected as follows:

1. The co-ordinating committee of representatives of participating community agencies shall establish operating agreements and policies.
2. General administration shall be under the direction of the General Assistant Superintendent of Schools.
3. An assistant to the principal shall be appointed by the Board of Education to direct the community center in each school.
4. The Board of Education shall pay all costs of operating buildings, the salaries of assistants to principals, and some of the adult education teachers.
5. All fees charged to those participating in the program shall be collected by the Board of Education, with the exception of fees charged for University of Minnesota extension courses

which may be offered in the community centers. Extension
courses at the college level for veterans may be an immediate necessity because of the crowded conditions at the University.

6. Other participating community organizations shall provide
personnel and services without charge to the Board of Education.

Community Centers Chosen

The highly delinquent area and the privileged area were
both rejected in selecting locations for community centers.
The committee agreed that it would be a mistake to open
centers in highly delinquent areas because there would not
be the response from parents that would be needed in the
beginning of such a project, and a privileged area probably
would not value the community center. Average communities were therefore selected. Over a period of years the
principal of the Jordan High School had made surveys of
delinquency, races, social centers, churches, schools—paro-
chial and public, in North Minneapolis—and could give
sound reasons for the Jordan School being chosen as a
logical location for the North Side Community Center.
The principal of the Bryant Junior High School had made
similar studies of the South Minneapolis location. Thus
the two schools, Jordan and Bryant Junior High, were
designated as community centers. Before the final decision
was made, the areas were carefully canvassed to ascertain
interests and needs of adults and older youth in each community. A study was made to assure adequate housing and
sufficient equipment to provide a broad program for those
attending.

According to an annual report of the Jordan Community Center,
"The director with the help and co-operation of the General
Assistant Superintendent of Schools, the principal of Jordan

Junior High School, and a Policy Board consisting of a representative from each co-ordinating agency, is directly responsible for the administration of the Community Center. The building staff consists of a clerk, receptionist, certified instructors from Minneapolis schools, lay workers, who teach special skills, Park Board and YMCA supervisors and teachers, volunteer workers who conduct forums and discussions, Red Cross instructors, club leaders and building maintenance men."

Both centers were opened October 7, 1946. The North Side Community Council became the local sponsoring group for the Jordan center.

First Beginnings

In Jordan Junior High School three small rooms were joined by removing their partitions to make room for a branch library with 15,000 volumes. The school library was merged with this branch, which is now open fourteen hours a day. The Park Board and the YMCA have joined in supporting an expanded program of sports and recreation for men, women, and young people. A game room, two gymnasiums, and the swimming pool are filled four nights of the week from 6:00 to 10:00 P.M. The Red Cross conducts classes in swimming, life-saving, cooking, and home nursing. On Friday nights boys and girls alternate with adults in the use of the school gymnasium for dancing directed by the Park Board instructors. One gymnasium is equipped with a public-address system so that an instructor can direct or teach the groups, or play records for dancing.

A community band for working boys and girls, supported by the North Side Athletic Association, practices twice a week and furnishes music for general programs conducted by the center. Child psychology classes for parents are sponsored by the Community Council's Co-ordinating Committee.

Offered also are public speaking by the Toastmasters' Club, photography by the Eastman Kodak Company, and courses in vegetable and landscape gardening sponsored by the Northrop King and Company, a large seed house. These few are mentioned to illustrate how business concerns and professional societies offer free services to the adult students.

There are nearly fifty adult groups meeting each week for which a course fee is charged, ranging from $1.75 to $3.00 for twelve to twenty-four hours of instruction. The 1,600 or more adults who are now participating in the program seem to want relaxation, a change of activities, and social enrichment.

Another adult department that is of wide public interest is the privilege of using the school auditorium for public discussions and concerts and the dining room for banquets, dinners, and luncheons. Examples are the annual Boy Scout "Court of Honor" banquet with 600 plates, the North Side Social Workers' luncheon for sixty agency workers held four times a year, a dancing school's annual show with 1,200 guests, and mass meetings conducted by the Community Council to extend better bus service to the citizens.

The youngsters of elementary school and junior high age are offered a sports and recreational program after school from 3:30 to 5:30 P.M., four days a week, and the Hi-Y boys take over on Friday.

Every community has young people who belong to no organized group. Some of them wander about the streets after dark and, of course, are attracted by the well-lighted school building. The hostess directs them to the game room presided over by an ex-G.I. who understands boys and girls. Here they may play ping-pong, table games, or just visit until the curfew time. They are guests of the Park Board.

Results

Within two years wide results could be seen. Vandalism decreased and fewer school windows were broken. There was a friendlier spirit among the school patrons. Citizens generally seemed to make efforts to show a friendlier spirit toward minority groups. A Negro artist conducted three classes one year. Twenty-eight white children were in his pottery class and eighteen white women in his sketching class. At the end of the season a tea was given in his honor as he exhibited his own and his students' work.

A study of the enrollments revealed a representation of many professions and vocations. Doctors, dentists, artists, teachers, politicians, skilled and unskilled workers, retired men and women, housewives, and others were taking advantage of the program. Within two years, enrollment climbed to over 57,000 persons. These figures are eloquent, but what community co-operation has done for the people is even more important.

PERSPECTIVE

There appear to be several over-all helpful ways in moving school community activities forward. The first of these is "to begin small," and to expand the project personnel and program as rapidly as possible. This sounds a bit like double talk but nearly all reports of community projects—and specifically the four here reported—bear out this statement. For example, the supervisor of rural schools initiated the Greenhow Community project but she soon perfected an organization representing all of the agencies working with rural people in the county. These workers composed a cross-section of personnel serving the county and included agricultural agents, the Home Demonstration Agent, and School Lunch Supervisor, the County Nurse, the vocational agricultural teachers in both the high school and the nearby state agricultural and mechanical college, and the County Superintendent of Public Instruction. Together they made up a planning council on a county-wide basis. Its weakness—later remedied—was the absence of interested lay people and the local teachers. When the supervisor had convinced the key people, listed above, of the possibility of the proposed program, the circle was widened to include the teachers. Finally, the circle was widened to include the children, and through them, the parents. Thus from a small beginning of an individual, the personnel expanded to include hundreds of people. Apparently strength for a project lies in such inclusion and thus should be accomplished as rapidly as the program will allow it.

The Manhasset project began small also. It began with a small curriculum committee, and expanded into a larger one which included many lay people. Too, the school community survey in Urbana grew out of joint professional-lay interest, was authorized by the school board, and quickly involved the university as well as townspeople, students, and faculty.

The report from Minneapolis emphasizes also the small beginning. Minneapolis wished to establish centers in all her communities, but wisely decided to experiment with two. This appears to be a sensible approach to the community problems in large metropolitan areas. The selection of pilot communities, the establishment of experimental programs in them, and the development of techniques which can be applied on a city-wide basis is a way of working which can bear study, and perhaps deserves imitation.

The second helpful practice which emerges from these reports is that children should understand that the experiences they have are really important to better community living. In nearly all of the projects, the activities were considered by the participants as intrinsically important. They were neither designed nor developed to teach children certain lessons vaguely seen as "good for them." It appears also that young people should be included at the planning stage of the community project. Apparently, the success with which the project moves forward depends upon this practice. The metropolitan study illustrates this point. The experiment in the two pilot communities was preceded by study, and significantly enough, the study was made by the graduating class of a junior high school. This was important because the study involved those aspects of the local community in which young people are interested, namely, the availability of social and recreational resources for the teen-age group of the community. The co-operation of the city-wide council of social agencies and the adolescents in a junior high school graduating class was certainly an auspicious way to begin a project which finally led to the establishment of seventeen community councils in the metropolitan area.

Third, a good practice to move community projects forward seems to be to find ways of expanding initial projects. This practice was noted in the chapter, *Getting Started* and was designed as on-going projects. In the Greenhow report it was stated that while the children were working on the project at school, adults interested in their children participated also. Participation expanded not only to include parents but also practice teachers from a near-by college and specialists in Scouting. As interest in the project widened more and more activities developed. For example, the major problem attacked in the Greenhow community was housing, but this soon expanded to include the modernization and beautification of the school and grounds, the inauguration of a recreation program, the organization of clubs and the improvement of eating habits with special emphasis on nutrition. School community co-operation in Greenhow has developed through more than ten years, and the results well justify the efforts of the children, as well as of the lay and professional groups. Manhasset's problem of developing a resource file for the school, as simple as this at first seems, was expanded to include six other problems to which the committee gave attention before the project was completed. By the same process of expansion the Urbana study included a comprehensive reading improvement program, and revision of the guidance, marking and reporting systems. In Minneapolis, the Jordan center began as a new branch library, but this, too, developed an expanded program of community services. One of the chief requisites of moving forward, therefore, seems to be in part the ability of leaders to increase constantly the areas of responsibility which can be accepted by as large a number of persons and organizations as possible.

Closely tied to the third, is the fourth good practice suggested by the reports on how communities move forward. This is the practice of securing participation of large numbers of people on projects. Apparently, as was suggested in a previous chapter, it is not enough to get people interested and concerned about a problem; they must be moved to take personal action about it. Moreover, as the reports in this chapter indicate, if projects move forward more and more people must act on their concerns. The Greenhow community is a good example of how this happens. The project began with the participation of one person, but, in the ten years covered by the report, practically all of the people in the community participated in one way or another in the solution of these problems. Examination of the Urbana and Minneapolis projects indicates also that the same widespread pattern of lay participation is basic to programs successfully moving forward.

Moreover, as participation increases some care should be taken in giving it form and structure. Co-operative community projects sometimes fail because their elements are neither co-operative nor co-ordinated. In nearly all the reports, efforts were made to secure both. In Urbana, for example, adequate provision was made from the outset for constant contact between the three central committees as well as for co-operation among the subcommittees of each. The need for co-ordination and co-operation of school and community is especially pressing in metropolitan areas. It presents indeed both a challenge and an opportunity. Large numbers of people create difficulties in communication and co-operation, but once a group begins to move like a team, power seems to be generated almost at once. The report from Minneapolis illustrates the validity of the above statements and demonstrates as well the techniques by which co-operation is furthered. In the Minneapolis report it is apparent that the Council of Social Agencies—an organization present by one name or another in nearly all cities—took the initiative. The initiative might just as well, however, come from the school board, or from the superintendent of schools or from the teachers or children. This seems an important principle in moving ahead. Responsibility for community-school work does not rest solely with school people. It is, in reality, the concern of everybody, and sometimes the most important function of educational leaders is to know when to follow community leadership instead of accepting leadership or expecting to lead.

Finally, it seems important to secure a sustained working leadership if community-school work is to move forward. One criticism frequently made, and sometimes justifiably so, is that community-school activities are often transitory and ephemeral. Critics frequently say that too often many of the dramatic, interesting activities of today are gone tomorrow, lost and forgotten even in the communities where they were once so important. The answer to these criticisms is to find ways to continue the work once it is well begun. A good technique is to see that the responsibility for moving forward is centered in designated people. Manhasset exemplifies one way in which this can be done—namely, by the appointment of standing and special committees composed of lay people and educators, responsible for seeing that the program continues and that it constantly and constructively expands.

5

Taking Stock

SOME TWO HUNDRED CASE studies or descriptions of community projects were examined in the writing of Part II. In general, all revealed a lack of evidence of evaluation. If these reports are typical, very few people engaged in community activities are making serious efforts to evaluate their practices. The accounts were sprinkled with such statements as "the pupils were greatly intrigued," or "this made a lasting impression on the children," or "the memory of this experience will last a lifetime," or "the community was inspired and enthusiastic." Both the exuberance of the reporters and the lack of evidence of the worthwhileness of the activities reveal a real weakness in the whole community-school program which should be closely scrutinized by its advocates.

The school is an on-going social institution and presents special problems in appraisal. This difficulty should be, in effect, a spur to action, rather than a deterrent of it. All community participation, no matter how sporadic or permanent, should be accompanied by honest, objective appraisal. Moreover, the evaluation should be continuous. The community which supports the school has a proper concern that its program pays adequate dividends on the investment. The staff, the parents, and the students have a very real and particular regard for the quality of the educational process, whether it be in a community school or not. If the school is life-centered, that is all the more reason that evaluation be engaged in continuously. The community school is still in an experimental stage; those engaged in the experiment should be willing and able to test the faith that is in them.

Moreover, advocates of the community school should be able to develop instruments which indicate both the quantity and the quality of the behavior of people in their attainment of established goals. Is one of the goals of a community school to help people—both children and adults —to work as a team, to develop "we-ness" and groupness; as together they seek to improve the quality of living? How can it be determined whether or not this goal is being attained, and if so, in what respects and to what degree? Is one of the objectives of the community school to develop in people democratic values of service? How measure this achievement? These are more difficult items to evaluate than to count the number of sanitary privies built, or to estimate the value of food produced in a school garden, but they are none the less important. Evaluation really all comes down to what the community wishes to accomplish, and to what degree the people can be satisfied with the means and the results of the process involved in attaining their objectives. In the last analysis, appraisal is passing judgment on a program in terms of goals, pertinent descriptions of what is being judged, and criteria to determine the quality and quantity of achievement. This is no easy task, but neither is it an impossible one.

IMPROVING LIVING
IN SCHOOL AND COMMUNITY [1]

The report which follows tells the story of the Norristown school and community. While both are small, the people—both lay and professional—were interested not only in making progress in the attainment of objectives but also in recording it. Thus a rather clear picture emerges, showing both the process of evaluation and the way its progress was recorded.

Norristown Community is a rural area located in the southwest section of Emanuel County, Georgia. Four general stores, a church, a theater which operates only on week ends, and a few homes make up the center of the community. The chief occupation of the community is farming; however, many farmers derive a portion of their income from forestry products. Forty-four families of the community are represented in the school.

The school is a wooden building consisting of three classrooms, an auditorium, a storage room, and a combination principal's office and library. A crude wooden structure behind the school building serves as a lunchroom. Drinking fountains and toilets are located outdoors.

At the beginning of the 1950-51 school term, the walls of the classrooms were dull, dirty, and unattractive. The dark colored paint, applied many years ago, was darkened still more by the accumulation of dust and smoke from the coal stoves which heated the rooms. The black chalkboards, well-

[1] This story was submitted by Joan B. White, Instructional Supervisor, Emanuel County Schools, Swainsboro, Georgia.

worn with use, darkened the rooms even more. The appearance of the school yard was even more discouraging. An erosion problem had developed and numerous gullies had been formed. This condition limited the play area. Several of the fence posts were down. The gate was off its hinges.

Seventy-three pupils, distributed from grades one through seven, and three teachers made up the personnel of the school. Only one of the teachers had taught in the Norristown School prior to this school year.

Exploring the Problem

Early in the school term the county instructional supervisor and the teachers began to work together in studying the school and community in order to plan and develop a program that would help to meet the needs of the pupils and people within the community. The study revealed the conditions described below:

1. The school curriculum was concerned largely with teaching subject matter outlined in textbooks.
2. There was a need for changes in instruction. There was little evidence of teacher-pupil planning or the use of problem-solving techniques.
3. The school yard was eroded; natural light inside the building was reduced greatly by dark walls and blackboards.
4. There was a need for becoming more familiar with and utilizing more effectively the resource people and agencies of the school and community.
5. Community participation in the school program was almost nonexistent.
6. The natural resources with the school and community were in need of conservation and further development.

As the survey of school and community problems was being made, the teachers, with the help of the supervisor, discussed such questions as, "How can we improve the ap-

pearance of the building?" "How can we improve the
appearance and usefulness of the school grounds?" "Who
can help with these problems?" "How can we use these experiences to improve teaching procedures?" "How can we
work at these problems so as to make some difference in
attitudes and practices of pupils in the school and of adults
in the community?"

To find answers to their questions the teachers soon became involved in studying, planning, and working with
pupils, community people, and agencies. Many conferences,
committee meetings, and group meetings were held to
develop an awareness of the existing problems. In the beginning the planning usually started with the staff and
supervisor and moved out to include pupils and lay persons. Later, some activities were initiated in the classrooms
and in organizations of the community.

The teachers accepted the opportunities of working with
pupils and lay persons as a challenge to develop a school
program that would make some difference in the lives of the
people served by the school. The teachers recognized a need
for professional help. They secured books, magazines, bulletins, films, and resource persons to point the way to desirable learning experiences for themselves, the pupils, and
the people of the community. Planning and developing a
school program based on the real problems of the school
and community was a different and more difficult procedure
than assigning pages in the arithmetic, geography, and history textbooks.

Activity Pattern

Planning and working on various projects such as controlling erosion on the grounds, painting the interior of the
building, and establishing a school forest followed a rather

definite pattern. This pattern included (1) recognition of a problem by one person or a small group; (2) helping others to recognize the problems; (3) planning with school and community groups to see what each could contribute to the solution of the problem; and (4) planning with resource persons and agencies who could help with the problem. With slight variations each problem attacked passed through these four stages of development.

As a result of school and community efforts during one nine-months school term many improvements were made in the building and on the grounds. The classrooms, auditorium, and halls were painted. The school yard was terraced and a permanent lawn was established. The fence was repaired. A wildlife border was planted. Shade trees were pruned and underbrush removed from the wooded area of the grounds. A cement walk was laid from the gate to the front entrance of the building. A new flag pole was erected and painted.

Community interest in the school increased during the year. The records of the secretary of the Parent-Teacher Association show an increase from twelve to sixty-six paid members during the school term. The county agent stated that the attendance at Farm Bureau meetings had tripled since that organization had begun to participate in the school improvement program. A two-way trend has developed in school and community meetings. Teachers and pupils have become participants in community organizations and parents have become participants in school planning groups.

Results Counted

Teachers' observations of pupils indicated an increased interest on the part of pupils in school work. Poor relationships have improved. Increased pride in school housekeeping has been exhibited by pupils. Care has been shown in keeping the newly painted walls clean and in keeping attractive flower arrangements in classrooms and in the hall.

Observations made by the supervisor, and guided by the *Ohio Teaching Record,* indicated several points wherein instruction has been improved. Teachers have increased the supply of supplementary materials by using additional pamphlets and other printed materials with the textbooks and library books. Wider use has been made of field trips. A school forest has been developed on a farm near the school for a long range study of forestry. Opportunities for inter-class visitation have been provided for the pupils during the school year. Creative arts have been developed to a much greater degree during the year. Increased use of visual aids has been made through films, maps, and charts. The teaching of reading, writing, and number skills has become a more functional procedure. Children have made considerable improvement in their ability to express themselves orally and in written form. Teachers and pupils have improved in their ability to plan together. Committee and group work have been developed as regular classroom procedures. Planned work experiences have been added to classroom activities.

Results of a questionnaire show that a carry-over has been made in the community during the year of the school-community program. Twelve families painted all or a portion of their homes. Sixteen families have done additional building on homes or farm buildings. Twenty-six families have made repairs on the farm or home. Fifteen families have planted shrubbery. Eleven families have planted cover crops on farm land. Ten families have planted some land with pines, and ten families have increased the amount of pasture land on their farms. Eight farmers have built terraces of the type built at school.

Near the end of the school term a meeting was held for school planning and for evaluation of the current year's work. Parents indicated the desire to continue and expand the type of school program that had been carried on during the year. They indicated that the program had aided in the growth and development of parents as well as pupils. The teachers felt that they had made considerable progress in developing a school program that did make some difference in the lives of the pupils and their parents.

LEADERSHIP AT WORK [2]

Some of the ways through which an imaginative and resourceful school administrator moved his school out of the traditional and into something of a community pattern are highlighted in this account covering 24 years of progress in Floodwood, Minnesota. This was truly a developmental program, not a previously blue-printed plan. Yet it steered from its beginning by the fundamental conviction that a job of the school is to help improve the quality of community living.

The community school at Floodwood developed not as the result of following a set pattern involving certain techniques of teaching and community relations, but through the discovery or awareness of community needs. As these needs were pointed up the school staff, the students, and the

[2] This account was written by Lewis E. Harris, who was teacher, principal, and superintendent at Floodwood, Minnesota, from 1925 until 1949. He is now Associate Director for the School-Community Development Study, part of the Kellogg Foundation-sponsored Co-operative Program in School Administration, Ohio State University.

people of the community resorted to a program of action, experimental in nature, in which several techniques were employed, traditional teaching methods were largely abandoned for a more democratic approach, and a new system of evaluation set up. The ways in which the needs were discovered and the program of action which followed with the school as a central co-ordinating agency largely determined the development of the school through a quarter-century of progress.

The impetus for an educational program to improve living standards came from the people themselves, from their leaders, and from the school through joint awareness of the newly-settled submarginal land, the depleted forests, the people unprepared for transition from one means of livelihood to another, and the poor financial condition of the local government as the result of low taxable valuation of land.

Development of Community Projects and Activities

Independent School District Number 19 included three townships and had a total enrollment of 372 (September, 1925) in its three rural schools and one central building in the village. The small town of 371 served as a hub for a rural area of twelve or more townships from which secondary students were drawn. By 1949 the village population had grown to 812, and 454 students were enrolled in the consolidated school district. The rural area with a population of more than 3000, the majority of whom were of the Finnish nationality, supplied more students than the small village.

The administrator who participated in the growth of the community-school program over a twenty-four year period,

1925-1949, learned to know the community as a teacher
the first two years, as a high school principal the third year,
and as superintendent the last twenty years. As teacher and
coach in a traditional school he became aware of the lack
of recreation in the community and so devoted much time
to arranging varied athletic and musical programs which
called youths and adults into active participation. The response from the people was enthusiastic; through the years
they provided encouragement for an ever-enlarging program of activities which enlisted the resourcefulness and
involvement of the school staff and of many adults. This
did much to build up from the beginning a good relationship between the school and its community.

The first deviation from the traditional type of teaching
came early in 1925 with the school's support and development of the community fair. In it the school staff saw opportunity to help farm people of the area learn about
improved agricultural practices. The first group to leave
the school premises to assist in the community fair project
was the manual training class whose help was solicited in
the building of shelves, booths for displays, and coops for
poultry.

In the twenty-four years which followed, the school became involved in numerous community projects such as
rural electrification, a co-operative creamery, and annual
promotion of the local community fair. Interest on the part
of the local creamery resulted in a co-operative educational
program to improve the quality of dairy stock through an
artificial insemination project and through cow-testing. Interest in propagating an extensive dairy program then stimulated development of quality milk with low bacterial count,
soil restoration, and conservation programs. The school
staff seized every opportunity to supplement and support
community enterprises. The school served as an experi-

mental laboratory in trying out new ideas such as artificial insemination of cattle, improved poultry housing, seed testing, milk testing, cow testing, and in developing calf and cattle-feed formulas. Adult education classes became a means of extending interest in the community in the ideas which grew out of experimentation in the school and in new ideas from outside sources, such as the University of Minnesota Experimental Stations. The needs for reforestation and recreation were met jointly through a school park project. This was later extended to include a 109-acre school forest. Health needs were recognized in the culmination of a hot lunch program which served every child in the school and in the building of a community cannery. An extensive music program was developed to help meet the cultural needs of the people.

Certain Factors Involved in the Development of the Floodwood Community-School Program

What factors were involved in the development of the community-school program at Floodwood? They were numerous and varied. Some were unique to Floodwood, others were general in nature. Some factors were apparent in the nature of the community itself. Some motivational forces were factors. Still others emerged from beliefs, ideals, and attitudes of the individuals and the groups involved. Many operational procedures themselves appeared to be factors of significance. Between these several factor fields may be considerable inter-relationship, but it is felt that all the items listed below did have unusual quality which really made a difference in bringing about the community-school program. These are "natural history" data resulting from common-sense observation and are now listed as such:

FACTORS DETERMINED BY THE NATURE
OF THE COMMUNITY

1. The unique nature of a young community with few educational traditions.
2. The geographical location of the community approximately forty miles distant from larger population centers.
3. The in-group feeling of a major nationality group in the community.
4. The presence in the community of a larger percentage of foreign-born who did not question the authority of the teacher and who showed the typical old-world respect for the teaching profession.
5. A low literacy rate in English among many parents of the school children.
6. The character of the community in occupational transition from the timber industry to farming, tradeswork or business.
7. The rapid growth of strong consumer and producer co-operatives during the period paralleling the development of the community-school program.
8. The health conditions of the community with a high percentage of tuberculosis, poor teeth, and dietary deficiency.
9. The narrow academic nature of the school curriculum in the early 1930's.
10. The village within the school district with a low annual tax income, insufficient to maintain normal public services.
11. The poor financial condition of the school district which called forth the creative efforts of the faculty to do the best possible work with a minimum of supplies, textbooks, and equipment. It challenged the administration to find new solutions to maintaining a program of education, and resulted in the realization by the people that they were paying a very small percentage of the cost of maintaining the school.
12. The improvement of the financial condition of individual families, business enterprises, and sub-divisions of government from a low economic status to a more satisfactory level from the years 1930 to 1949.
13. The legal independence of a school board in an independent school district.

MOTIVATIONAL FORCES DETERMINED THE
FOLLOWING FACTORS

1. A variety of means were available where people could "have their say" and express their ideas. This was true for the students, the teachers, and the members of the community through the student council, school board meetings, agricultural planning councils, teachers' union, village council, civic club, political clubs, faculty meetings, church councils, and town board meetings.

2. The social drive of certain people caused them to compete for status through community leadership activities.

3. The community leadership roles of certain board members motivated acceptance and community support for various school and community activities.

4. The creative talents of certain members of the school faculty made a positive difference in the development of the community-school program.

5. The co-operative spirit of the pioneer settlers was shown when they helped to build each others' churches and when they patronized each others' benefits.

6. The experiences of Finnish-born people in their struggle against church-state domination in Finland may have been a force in their support of democratic developments.

7. The attempt on the part of the local timber and mercantile company through the 1930's to dominate the business and political life of the community which resulted in the resistance and unification of co-operative and liberal-minded people.

8. Conflicts occurred between private business and the co-operatives. Furthermore, there were internal differences within the co-operatives. In both these conflict situations there was the tendency to make a scapegoat of the school.

9. Competition between the co-operative organizations and private businesses caused conflicts which extended into the field of recreation. The interest developed in backing athletic teams was utilized to stimulate a community recreation program resulting eventually in unified community effort.

10. There was a strong liberal majority of voters in each of the voting precincts of the community after 1930.

11. National organizations sponsoring local attacks on schools may have contributed to the opposition to the general education program.

12. Few commercial recreational activities were available in the community, so young and old were eager to take part in organized recreational and social activities.

13. The community needed a meeting place and the school was for years the only available space.

14. There was a feeling of acceptance and security on the part of the teachers and nonprofessional employees as the result of tea and coffee sessions in the superintendent's office, picnics and parties at his home, and at the homes and lake cottages of members of the faculty.

15. There was the attitude of "try it" on the part of the administration when suggestions were made or new ideas advanced.

16. Certain faculty members and the superintendent were affiliated with the Allied Teachers Guild, a liberal educators' group which helped to formulate a progressive educational philosophy in the early 1930's.

17. The organization of Local No. 506, American Federation of Teachers, appeared to make a difference in the interest which teachers took in planning and development of an expanded program.

18. A study of the 186 teachers employed during the twenty-five year period revealed that the 32 teachers identified with "creative teaching" had longer tenure than the average teacher in the system.

19. The somewhat extended tenure of certain members of the Board of Education provided the assurance of continuity in developing the community educational program.

FACTORS DETERMINED BY BELIEFS, IDEALS
AND ATTITUDES

1. There was the feeling in the community "We can do something about it" in regard to any problem, whether in the school, civic affairs, or the co-operatives.
2. The honesty, integrity, and the earnestness of the people were factors in any community endeavor.
3. The school board was willing to accept suggestions from other groups and individuals in the community.
4. An attitude of acceptance prevailed on the part of the superintendent and the board toward the unique habits, attitudes, beliefs, and individual characteristics of teachers on the staff.
5. The school board and the superintendent believed in the desirability of setting up every possible opportunity for democratic experiences.
6. There was a fundamental belief on the part of the faculty and the administration in the extension and development of democracy through the educative process.
7. The attitude existed on the part of the superintendent, principal, and certain faculty members that the state course of study was not infallible, nor was it to be slavishly followed; that the faculty of the local school working together with the students and the parents had the intelligence to adequately plan the learning experiences to be included in a program of community education.
8. The administration of the school was willing to take the risk involved in trying new projects.

OPERATIONAL FACTORS

A considerable number of factors could be classified as operational in nature. Some of these are related to motivational forces and a few are related to those listed as beliefs, ideals, and attitudes. In one or two cases these factors may seem more like results than causes. But a result can give a new impetus to a program, and thus itself become a causal factor. There is a circular relationship among all the factors listed which tends to make the program of community education grow like a snowball. These operational factors give some specific clues to how a community-school program is developed:

1. A co-operative working relationship developed between community organizations on such projects as the community fair, Independence and Memorial Day observances, and in war-service activities.
2. There was a high degree of co-operative interaction between the school and many community organizations such as the Fair Association, Civic Club, American Legion, Floodwood Co-operative Creamery Association, The Parent-Teachers Association, the Village Council, and the Floodwood Co-operative Association.
3. The organization of advisory councils kept the educational program close to the needs of the community and the organization of the parent study club promoted understanding of the purposes of the general education program.
4. Teachers were active in community activities and organizations.
5. An open and co-operative relationship was maintained with the churches: joint meetings of the clergymen in planning week-day release of time for students' religious instruction; a minister acting as Scout master for a troop sponsored by the school.
6. As groups in the community developed skill in group action they were encouraged to provide their own leadership.
7. The school encouraged other community organizations to take over experimental programs investigated and tried out by the school, such as the artificial insemination program taken over by the creamery.
8. The school building was constantly used by teachers, students, parents, community groups, and recreational-social groups.
9. The administration of the school maintained an open-door policy so teachers felt free to go to the superintendent's office for an idea conference or just for a friendly chat.

10. An operational factor which may also be regarded as a belief was the willingness of the administration to make use of conflict as a method of resolving difficulties.

11. The superintendent was active in political, co-operative, fraternal, and educational affairs in and outside the community from which benefits accrued to the community in the form of work projects, school funds, special school legislation, co-operation from state and county highway departments, and other state agencies.

12. A close relationship was maintained by the superintendent and certain staff members by attendance and help at births, weddings, sickness and death in the community. Personal relationships were also promoted through fishing and hunting outings with people in the community.

13. Members of the faculty took an active interest in statewide teachers' associations, the American Federation of Teachers, Group Health Mutual, Secondary Principals' Association, and in state and national political organizations.

14. Teachers were deliberately selected for their unique qualifications and for individual competencies which would lend a wide variety to the staff.

15. The teachers worked together and with the administration to plan the curriculum and the policies of the school.

16. After the teachers' union was organized there was a healthy co-operation between the faculty and the school board over such items as teachers' salary schedules, wage levels, curricular program, school calendar, and educational legislation.

17. The Board of Education adopted the practice of inviting members of the community, teachers and other school workers to attend board meetings. Delegations who had matters to present usually sat through all of the meeting.

18. The Board of Education usually approved the recommendations of the superintendent with a strong majority.

19. The policies of the Board of Education gradually changed from approval of a narrow academic program to approval of a broad program of community education.

20. The Board of Education progressively raised the qualifications of the teachers to be hired.

21. An early step in encouraging students to stay in school was the elimination of eighth-grade graduation and the adoption of a junior high exploratory program (1936).
22. A permissive atmosphere pervaded the school and the community.

The data do not permit quantitative analysis of the many factors discussed above. In examining the history of the program it appears that none of the factors stand alone but that, taken together, they represent those forces which produced a community-school program at Floodwood.

Identifying and Meeting Community Needs

The awareness and insight needed by the faculty to become sensitive to conditions of living in the community developed as a result of experiences in the community itself. This appeared to be a gradual process with recognition of one need leading to further understandings. This was accelerated when the school began to survey case studies of families in need of relief, to secure data for the Rural Electrification Administration in application for the building of power lines in the rural areas, and for school-aid grants. These data pointed up many needs around which the school program was planned. Class diet surveys, dental and physical examinations of each child, a farm survey, a well survey, and a hospital survey suggested health needs.

Teachers who made drop-out reports followed them up by visiting the homes to ascertain the causes. This led to discovery of new interests and attitudes around which the staff tried to build the school program.

Teachers were encouraged to attend and participate in community organizations so as to gain new insights into the thinking of the people.

Teachers were hired who appeared to have social sensitivity; they discovered many of the needs of the children and the adults as they worked and played with them in their homes and at school.

Evaluating the Program

Teachers shared in evaluating the school program as they became more and more involved in planning the curriculum. The interest of the teachers themselves was in effect an evaluation of the program. Although no definite pattern of approach is clearly discernible, an examination of the development of the program of studies and the school and community projects in which the school participated seems to indicate the general terms by which assessment of the program was made.

In general it can be said that the program was evaluated as to its success in meeting the needs of the youths and adults of the community—and particularly as it helped to raise the level of living in the community. It must be admitted that many of the judgments of the staff were subjective in nature. One of the glaring defects in the program shows up at this point in that sufficient foresight was not possessed by anyone in the school to secure some immediate baseline data which could be used later for comparative purposes.

Teachers shared in evaluating the program in terms of:

BEHAVIORAL CHANGES IN STUDENTS

In 1936 teachers began to talk about changing the method of evaluating pupil progress and reporting to parents. It was two years later before they made specific recommendations to the board that each child be marked in terms of his own ability. As time went on there was greater emphasis on "attitudes, habits, and characteristics." The changes made in the marking system reflected to some degree how the teachers attempted to evaluate the behavioral changes of the students, and reflected also their understanding of learning and how it occurs.

STUDENT AND TEACHER EVALUATION OF
UNITS OF STUDY

At the culmination of each teaching unit or project the students in the general education groups wrote summaries giving their personal evaluation of work completed. This was duplicated and a copy placed in the permanent record folder of each student and filed in the principal's office. These records were found useful for the following year's teacher as the complete summaries provided a method of reviewing the scope of the work completed each year. These were student evaluations and contained many suggestions as well as criticisms of each project. They also included a statement of value derived from the activity. Taken together, these reports gave the teacher an over-all class evaluation.

A TESTING PROGRAM

Intelligence tests were administered every year in grades one, three, six, nine and twelve. Diagnostic tests in reading and arithmetic were used in the elementary grades, the junior high school, and in some of the general education classes in the senior high school. Aptitude and interest tests were used in connection with units on vocations in the ninth and eleventh grades. The Iowa GED Battery was administered in grades nine and ten. Some of the other tests used by teachers for a special purpose were tests of personality, critical thinking, interests, college aptitude and achievement in subject-matter areas. Reports written by teachers recognized that tests available from commercial sources failed to meet the objectives of the school program. Their chief value was to allow comparison to meet local criticism. In spite of the nonacademic nature of some of the school work, the Floodwood students compared favorably with national averages.

TEACHERS' REPORTS

Teachers evaluated the projects in which they were engaged through giving detailed reports to the entire faculty and to the Board of Education. As the reports were presented additional suggestions and appraisals were often given.

Curriculum reports were made monthly and annually for the Six-School Curriculum Development project, and were considered by the faculty as a part of the process of evaluation of the final program. In the introduction to the student and faculty curriculum report for 1948-49 it was stated, "This report should be studied for the purpose of evaluating the work done here this year." The preceding year the annual report summarized the opinions and comments of the students and the teachers in a list of twenty-two statements covering almost every phase of the program.[3] These were followed by a faculty résumé of "Successes and Shortcomings," a list of fourteen evaluative statements.

[3] Students and Faculty, *Final Curriculum Report, 1947-48*, Floodwood Community School.

THE SUPERINTENDENT'S MONTHLY REPORT

The superintendent made a detailed report to the Board of Education each month in which the board was informed of the progress of the work in school, and board members were called upon for suggestions. It was customary for the administrator to present a personal evaluation of the work being done by the various staff members, especially that which deviated from the traditional type of school program. Thus the faculty, the administration and the board worked as a unified and understanding body.

ADULT STUDY GROUPS

Large numbers of out-of-school youths and adults participated in adult education programs carried on in answer to local requests. The projects covered a wide field of activities including new methods in farming, carpentry, welding, electrical training, building and repair of farm machinery, improved dairy practices, health needs, hobbies, a broad musical program, folk dancing, drama, citizenship classes, and the formation of parent study clubs, the latter motivated by the desire to learn more about the general education program to which the school was turning.

SIX-SCHOOL CURRICULUM DEVELOPMENT PROJECT

In the fall of 1946 the school became associated with the Six-School Development project sponsored jointly by the University of Minnesota's College of Education and the State Department of Education. The following summer a group of six faculty members from the Floodwood school attended a curriculum workshop of the six schools at the university's summer session. There they worked out a cur-

riculum bulletin to be used as a basis for discussions at the
one-week planning conference of all the faculty, held prior
to the opening of school.

This bulletin contained the suggestion that the elementary
teachers continue the practice of reporting pupil progress
to parents by personal letter, a practice which had been
carried out the preceding year in grades one, two and three.
It was suggested that this be extended through the fourth
grade, and a grade beyond each succeeding year until the
practice was common throughout the six-year elementary
school. The elementary teachers adopted this procedure.

The committee was not able to make a complete list of
recommendations for evaluation of the secondary school
students' work. It was agreed that this subject would have
general discussion at the planning conference to be followed
by intensive work on the problem as the school year progressed and as the program developed.

The conference further agreed that no uniform methods
for evaluation of pupil progress be adopted, and that each
report sent home be different as to content and basis of
evaluation. Appraisal was to be made of progress rather
than of comparative status, in terms of developing work
attitudes, social qualities, and desirable characteristics of
good citizens. It was stated that emphasis in evaluation be
placed on progress in work and in learning as defined by
"change in behavior."

ORGANIZATION OF PLANNING COUNCILS

Adults in the community were called upon to help in the
planning of certain curriculum projects by serving on
planning councils. Such groups were composed of representatives from the faculty, the school board, school administration, students, and people of the community. Meetings

were always open, well advertised, and called on all interested for suggestions and services. The councils were found especially useful in planning various agricultural and recreational programs on a year-round basis. The interest of the individuals participating in project developments stimulated that of others, and so was utilized as a definite promotional technique.

NOTING PUBLIC ACCEPTANCE OR REACTION

In order to gauge public acceptance of a program teachers were on the alert for such evidence. This was gained through the use of student polls, parental conferences, school election campaign material, and from faculty contacts with the people of the community. The efforts made by the teachers to become a part of the community placed them in a better position to evaluate the total impact of the program of education in the community. As the teachers participated in planning they felt themselves more and more a part of a dynamic program. At all times the opinions of the students carried weight along with those of the people of the community.

CO-OPERATION
PAYS DIVIDENDS [4]

This is more than the story of a small town, how it improved through education, and evaluated its own improvement. It is the story of the town, but of its countryside also: of a county in Louisiana that is half-

[4] Based on a report by E. J. Niederfrank, Extension Rural Sociologist, United States Department of Agriculture.

way between Baton Rouge and New Orleans, lies astride the Mississippi River, and is called Ascension Parish.

In Ascension Parish the land along the river is rich and black, good for growing rice, sugar cane, and corn. The farms in this section of the parish are large—from 200 to 500 acres. On the east side of the river, however, the land is less productive, and the farms are small. These produce strawberries, vegetables, and other truck, but they cannot support all the people who live on them. In this area, one or two people work off the land; others in the sugar mills, on the river plantations, and in industry as far away as Baton Rouge.

Ascension is essentially a rural parish. The rural people, composing 92 per cent of the total population, live in the villages and on the farms in the open country. The urban population lives in Donaldsonville, a small town of about four thousand people, which is the county seat. In 1945 the total population differed little from that in 1900—about 22,500. All governmental agencies, including the schools, are administered by the parish. There are two important governing bodies, the parish police jury and the parish school board, composed of citizens elected from the several wards of the parish. There are five consolidated schools for white children in Ascension Parish and eleven country schools for Negroes. The one Negro school in Donaldsonville is also a high school.

When the parish began its improvement program in 1942, the living standards of the people were generally low, the parish Health Unit was understaffed, dietary habits were poor, most farmers had no conception of a live-at-home program, small scale farmers were in general ignored, and the schools were traditional and textbook-centered. These

well-recognized weaknesses in the parish became in effect
the point of attack and their remedies the goals in the improvement program. Emphasis in the program finally narrowed down to (a) the improvement of nutrition, (b) the
raising of health standards of the school children, especially as they related to their eyes and teeth, and (c) the
development of a live-at-home farm production program.

Common Goals

Leaders in the parish could have taken many ways to
attain the objectives listed above. Each organization interested in the improvement of living might have gone its way
alone, as is often the case, with resulting rivalries and confusion. Happily, a co-ordinated program was developed
instead. The idea originated with the parish superintendent
of schools and was advanced by him in 1942. This was a
war year, and the superintendent, acting as chairman of the
parish Nutrition Committee, concluded that if anything
more than talk was to happen, the various service agencies
of the parish would have to co-operate in a plan of action.
No effort was made to organize the agencies into a final
committee or a council. There were no officers and no
formalized procedures. Rather, there seemed to develop
from many conferences a consensus that all agencies should
work informally together under the leadership of the parish
superintendent of schools. Their common goal was to bring
about the improvement of rural living through education.
As the program developed other groups and agencies, both
local and state, were utilized. The most formal feature of
the co-operative plan was that meetings of the representatives of the several agencies were held from time to time,
generally in connection with some phase of the school
program.

In November 1946, agreement had been reached on the following overall and general parish objectives:

1. To improve rural life in all its phases.
2. To fully develop both natural and human resources.
3. To improve health through nutrition, sight, speech, and oral hygiene.
4. To improve housing and sanitation.
5. To increase co-operation among schools, agencies, and communities.
6. To establish a parish library.
7. To interpret activities and programs to the public.

Procedures used to achieve these objectives were:

1. Conferences and meetings.
2. Work-conferences.
3. Administration and supervision of instruction.
4. Study of techniques and materials.
5. Research and evaluation.
6. Clinics.
7. Individual contacts.
8. Demonstrations.

The agencies participating in these procedures were Parish School Board, Extension Service, Parish Health Unit, Parish Department of Public Welfare, Veterans Farm Training Supervisor, Production and Marketing Administration, clubs, churches and citizens, State Department of Education, State Department of Health, State Department of Public Welfare, Louisiana State University and Experiment Station, and the General Education Board. Co-ordination of these agencies was maintained through joint project committees, the annual teachers work-conferences, and co-operation in special projects, such as 4H Achievement Day, the FFA community fairs, and community canning.

The story of the co-operative program is too long to repeat here.[5] In order to provide a framework for our account, however, its achievements with their evaluation will be considered together under the basic goals of the whole program.

GOAL I: THE IMPROVEMENT OF NUTRITION

In order to attack the poor eating habits characteristic of the parish, a nutritional study was inaugurated by the Agricultural Experiment Station at Louisiana State University, with the co-operation of the General Education Board. The study was established to discover the best ways to teach nutrition as a means of improving health. It was begun in the schools. Teachers and pupils kept weekly records of their food intake for a week, and then scored them for their protective food value. Teachers, children, and parents did the scoring, and the self-analysis proved a fine learning experience for all who participated. Diet deficiencies showed up in the survey, especially that in Vitamin C and the dairy products, whole grain cereals, and red meat.

Teachers and children attacked this problem in the school through instruction. Nutrition was correlated with all regular class work—in spelling, writing, arithmetic. Geography classes studied where desirable foods were grown. Science and agriculture classes developed school gardens with emphasis on desirable foods. The home economics girls specialized on the survey data and the improvement of health through food. Art classes made posters, recipe booklets for the mothers, and illustrated stories on nutrition, home sanitation, etc. School lunch personnel, as they learned more about nutrition, put their knowledge to work, so that the point value of lunches began to rise.

[5] The story in full is available in the pamphlet by E. J. Niederfrank, *The Co-ordination of Agencies in Ascension Parish, Louisiana, to Improve Rural Living Through Education*. Louisiana State University, Baton Rouge, Louisiana.

In their summer workshops the teachers specialized on
materials in nutrition and health. They learned how to distinguish nutritious foods, and how to interest children in
them. Resource people came from the co-operating agencies
to assist with these problems so that a team attack developed.

Two years after the research and action programs had
been in operation the results attained were gratifying. The
point value of the school lunches had risen from 3.0 to 7.2.
Desirable and nutritious foods had replaced doubtful ones
on the lunch menus. Whole-wheat bread, carrots, oranges,
greens, eggs, and milk appeared. Improvement in the diets
of the school children for the years 1944-1946 follow.

PERCENTAGE RATING OF FOOD HABITS OF SCHOOL CHILDREN IN
FIVE WHITE SCHOOLS IN ASCENSION PARISH, LOUISIANA,
DECEMBER 1944-1946

	Per Cent	
	1944	1946
Good	1.5	21.4
Fair	57.0	69.6
Poor	41.5	9.0

PERCENTAGE RATING OF FOOD HABITS IN LOWREY TRAINING
SCHOOL (NEGRO), DONALDSONVILLE, LOUISIANA,
DECEMBER 1944-1946

	Per Cent	
	1944	1946
Good	0.0	2.2
Fair	8.2	29.3
Poor	91.8	68.5

GOAL II: TO IMPROVE THE HEALTH STANDARDS OF CHILDREN, ESPECIALLY AS RELATED TO EYES AND TEETH

A concentrated attack was made in the parish to widen its health program. The agencies co-operating here were those of Public Welfare and the Health Unit. Here again, in workshops and through in-service education, the teachers were given training in examining eyes, teeth, and the general health of children. As defects were found, parents were consulted and follow-up work was planned. School principals provided group transportation to clinics and to doctors and dentists.

The results indicate what can happen when public health officials are treated as partners instead of outsiders in a school health program. Within two years, the number of corrections of defects made at the school's suggestion rose from 89 to well over 6,000.

GOAL III: TO DEVELOP A LIVE-AT-HOME FARM-PRODUCTION PROGRAM

If education is a process which can affect adults as well as children, it is impossible to achieve Goals I and II above without happily affecting parents. Children eating the nutritious lunches at school discussed them at home. Nutrition problems began to appear on the programs of the home demonstration clubs. Two new clubs developed out of the need to understand foods. The Extension Service reported from three to four times as many requests as were usually received for information on gardening, cows, chickens, and pigs. Agricultural and extension agencies promoted the idea of winter gardens, possible in Louisiana because of the mild climate, and school surveys indicated real gains in the establishment of these home gardens. A community canning center and feed mill were installed in one school by the Vocational Agriculture Department. Dozens of canning demonstrations were held.

Business people become interested when school-community programs are vital. A local bank developed a plan to finance dairy heifers, on easy terms, for club work. Over three hundred pure-bred dairy heifers were raised in the parish during a three-year period by boys and girls on small farms.

Through the co-operative efforts of the several agencies home improvements, especially in those of Negroes, began to make their appearance. Screens, deep wells, and other sanitation improvements were added to 90 per cent of the homes of Negroes in two of the three communities studied. The coming of REA to the parish had a highly salutary effect.

A report from the U. S. Department of Agriculture summed up the co-operative efforts discussed in the previous paragraphs as follows:

All in all, the school teachers, agency workers, pupils, ministers, businessmen, and rural families of all economic levels are more conscious than before of nutrition, health, and welfare. They are doing something about it as fast as they can. The school program has been broadened and is more functional. Reading, 'riting, and 'rithmetic are still taught, but with reference to the life and experiences of the pupils. All the agencies—Extension Service, Public Welfare, Public Health, and the school system— have obtained some new visions, and their work is being turned to higher objectives. As one agency representative said, "We don't call on or bashfully ask other agencies for things like we used to; now, there is a feeling of being on the same team." And said the school teachers, "Yes, the teacher is just as busy under our new set-up but the things she does are different from ordinary; and teaching is a lot more interesting."

TEACHERS STUDY COMMUNITY LIVING[6]

We report finally how the teachers in the Baltimore city schools studied their community, how they used what they found in improving the curriculum experiences of their students, and how their information and concern about community problems were positively and directly reflected in Baltimore itself.

How the Program Developed

The Baltimore in-service program of community study was started in the fall of 1946. The program was planned for one afternoon every other week from 3:30 to 5:30 P.M. for a period of fifteen weeks. Participation was made possible for all teachers in all grades. During the first year of the study, sixty-five teachers enrolled and the meetings were experimental, all being planned by a committee of participants and the co-ordinator of the project. The fifteen meetings included trips to churches of different faiths, lectures on housing, and excursions to public housing projects and slum areas.

In May 1947, permission was granted by the Board of Superintendents to subsidize part of the expenses of eleven

[6] Reported by Harry Bard, Curriculum Bureau, Community Study Co-ordinator, Baltimore Public Schools. The program is described in detail in Bard's doctoral thesis, *Development and Evaluation of the Baltimore Teachers In-Service Community School Program.* College Park, Maryland: The University of Maryland, 1951.

See also his *Teachers and the Community: An In-Service Program in Action,* an Intergroup Education Pamphlet published by the National Conference of Christians and Jews, 381 Fourth Ave., New York City.

members of the study group to attend a two-weeks' workshop in community study at Wayne University in Detroit. During this workshop a manual was prepared describing the organization and procedure of the proposed comprehensive Baltimore teachers' in-service community study program.

That fall the program was richer because of the guidance found in the workshop at Wayne University, while the manual prepared there helped give direction to the whole group. Practically all of the sixty-five participants in the first year of the study remained with the group for the second year, and a new first-year group of 175 participants was organized.

In the spring of 1948 the Planning Committee again evaluated the program and arranged a one-week summer workshop in Baltimore for the purpose of training more leaders for the rapidly expanding program and for the purpose of enriching the sociological background of all interested participants. This summer workshop was not a required program for community study participants, but was primarily an enrichment activity for interested persons. The workshop was held in August 1948, during the week previous to the opening of schools. Much attention was given to the third-year program that was to come into being for the first time during the coming school year.

In September a new first-year group of about 200 teachers was organized, and the 200 participants of earlier years moved into the second- and third-year programs, making a grand total of 400 for the program during the school year 1948-49. In that year most of the energies were directed toward the new third-year program. Here the group found particularly valuable the plan developed at the August workshop, namely, to have attached to each third-year group a community consultant who was a specialist in the field. For example, the director of the Recreation Division of the

Council of Social Agencies met regularly with the Recreation Group that year. Similarly, the director of the Baltimore International YWCA was consultant for the Intercultural Group. While these consultants served without honorarium, other advisors were brought in for single meetings and often paid from the budget allotted the community study program.

By 1948 the program had grown so large in scope and enrollment that the Planning Committee felt there should be ongoing relationships with some educational authorities, preferably at the university level, who would help the participants recognize the major objectives of school-community relations and aid those in leadership roles to take care of the rapidly increasing enrollment. After some study it was decided to invite the College of Education and the College of Special and Continuation Studies at the University of Maryland to provide the workshop with this assistance. In November, 1948 these arrangements were completed and the university agreed to offer consultant help to the workshop. These co-operative efforts between the Baltimore schools and the university strengthened the community study program and brought many advantages to teacher participants.

In August 1949 another one-week enrichment workshop was organized primarily for the purpose of training leaders, evaluating the program and revising it accordingly. As a secondary aim, the workshop sought to give all those who felt the need for sociological material a short advanced course in "The City—Its Structure and Problems."

That year enrollment went up to 600 participants. Revisions were made in the existing programs, and two innovations were added. The first was the initiation of a seminar or fourth-year program, begun largely at the request of those who had finished three years of community study and who had an individual problem which they wanted to attack at the research and action level. About 30 teachers whose original membership had been with the first group of 65 were enrolled. A specialist acted as consultant to this group and helped them to use research techniques. The second innovation was that of the so-called "school groups." These groups were made up of ten to fifteen teachers in the same school who wanted to attack a school-community problem unique to them and to revise the curriculum accordingly. Five such groups were organized, each of which published its report at the end of the year's work.

In August, 1950 an advanced theory enrichment workshop was conducted under the direction of a Johns Hopkins specialist. Here the emphasis was again on leadership training and on evaluation of the program. About 200 teachers attended this workshop, among them being twenty-eight who were to have leadership roles the following year.

The year 1950-51 found nearly 780 teachers enrolled in the three years of the workshop and the seminar. These teachers represented practically every one of the 135 elementary and secondary schools in the city. The Planning Committee thought it would be well not to add any major features to the program during this year, but to concentrate on evaluation and to consolidate gains over the five-year period.

Aims of the Program

This community study program underscores three C's in its objectives:

Child acculturation—understanding the environmental and cultural influences that affect the child in his relation to the school and to learning.

> *Curriculum revision*—working with students, community leaders, parents and others to bring about learning that has meaning and purpose in terms of the child's developmental tasks and his societal needs.
>
> *Community action*—working with community agencies for the improvement of the child's environment and toward social progress.

Of course the participants in community study do not achieve all these aims during the first year of the program. Indeed, some of them never attain all the objectives. This is true of every in-service program reaching large numbers. On the other hand, most of the participants achieve some of the goals early in the first year of the program and during each succeeding year make additional progress. In general, teacher understanding of a community, awareness and use of community resources, and child acculturation comes rather early in the program. For most participants these gains occur during the first year of participation. On the other hand, significant curriculum revision usually starts during the second year of participation. Community action programs, with the school playing a leading role, however, are not likely to take place until the third year of participation or until the seminar in the fourth year.

This general pattern of progress is not the same for all teachers. In the case of one teacher, child acculturation always remains the most important aim; for another, curriculum revision or community action is of major concern through all four years of community study. Thus the program affects teachers in different ways, but it apparently affects them all to a significant degree.

Moreover, as participants remain in the program there is a sequence of progression. The detailed description of the scope of the program indicates a general progression in understanding the relationships between school and community, and in attaining the skills and techniques involved. The community study program obviously does not contain the fine elements of progression which are inherent in the study of mathematics as one moves from arithmetic to calculus. This could not be true because in community study the participants are people with varying backgrounds of understanding and the content is an ever-dynamic society. On the other hand, there is a progression of activity and study which has been planned to move the uninitiated through activities involving increasing understanding and effectiveness as participants move from the first year through the seminar experiences.

Sequence of the Program

Thus the first year of the program is concerned with understanding the community. The early experiences, such as the slum excursions, are planned with the view to shock participants into realization of how little they know of the community in which they teach. Similarly, the visits to churches of different faiths help teachers to see early in the program how intimately religious culture patterns affect their pupils. The same holds true of the interracial meetings. Moreover, analysis of census data, inventories of the community resources, and population-composition reports are stressed during the first year to bring about a richer understanding of the community in which the teacher lives and works. Teacher attitudes toward the community, and toward the environmental influences affecting the pupil, are often changed in the first year of the program. Guided, first-hand experience is the cause.

The second year is concerned largely with curriculum revision and with use of community resources. It is for this reason that in the second year of the program participants are asked to concentrate their efforts in one problem area of interest. For example, those who were working in the Historical Resources Group in 1950-51 visited the Peale Museum, the Maryland Historical Society, the Flag House, the Hampton Home and other patriotic shrines. Participants in this group wrote papers dealing with the use of these community resources in terms of their teaching assignments. In many cases, and only a short time after they themselves had taken the trips, teachers arranged for their own classes to visit these historical centers. Participants in the Industrial Group cited similar relationships to curriculum procedures after they had visited places like the Bendix Company and Lever Brothers. The same could be said of second-year participants in the Communications Group, the Recreational Group, and the Health Resources Group. Thus it developed that new information gained by teachers and new relationships with community resources changed the teaching situation and the curriculum for most participants.

The third year is concerned mainly with community action resulting from closer relationships between school and community. Now participants are asked to select an area in which they as individuals, or with others in the same school, can bring about important community improvements. For example, in 1950-51 third-year participants in the Intercultural Group co-operated with the National Conference of Christians and Jews in planning Brotherhood Week and with the Urban League in celebrating Negro History Week, not only in the schools but in the city as a whole. Third-year participants in the various school groups stressed improvements in community recreational facilities, in housing situations, and in other areas where the school and community working together could bring about civic change. That is why techniques of working with agencies and lay persons, and content in group dynamics, are important aspects of the third-year program.

The seminar or fourth year is for participants who have acquired those attitudes, backgrounds and techniques which come after three years of participation and who have a special problem in school-community relations. The seminar stresses use of research and active relationships between school and community bearing on a particular problem. For instance, seminar participants in 1950-51 worked on such special action problems as how to get community help in developing a neglected city-owned lot into a school recreational spot, how to organize city youth councils in each Baltimore school, and how to initiate a school-wide inter-group education program. They also worked on such special research problems as collecting and interpreting data on adult education needs met by community groups in Northwest Baltimore, measuring community feeling about the United Nations, and understanding foster children who are enrolled in the Baltimore schools. In each case the problem is a real one which the teacher brings to the seminar and on which he expects help from all participants. For these reasons seminar sections are usually limited to fifteen participants.

Some participants are permitted to take the first and second year concurrently. This is possible since the two programs meet on alternate Tuesdays and Thursdays. Moreover, it is even advisable for a few teachers to come into the program with some previous background. These are able to enter the second-year program, which brings the participant into a specialized problem area. No participant may take the third-year program until he has fully completed the second-year work, nor may he take the seminar unless he has fully completed the third-year's program. Thus the minimum time to complete the full program is three years; most participants take four years. At no time, however, are participants made to feel that they must stay with the program for the four years. While each year is integrated with the others, it also has unity in its own right and teachers are permitted to drop out of the program after one or more years and still get their salary increment credit. More than 85 per cent, however, do stay for three or four years, and only a few drop out after one year.

Taking Stock

Evaluation of the program was begun early and has been continuous. Evaluation sessions took place the year the program was initiated, at the end of which each of the 65 first participants was asked to comment on different aspects of the program and to make suggestions for changes. In the summer of 1947, when 11 participants studied at Wayne University, much time was given to the analysis of what had been accomplished the first year and what improvements might follow. Each summer enrichment-program from 1947 to 1950 gave two or three sessions to the subject of evaluation. During each school year scheduled time was set aside for periodic evaluations to be held by first-, second-, and third-year groups and by the seminar. In addition, school and problem area groups had their own evaluative meetings. Evaluation has thus not been a separate phase of the program, but has been interwoven with the initiation, development, and expansion of activities. In 1950, however, a comprehensive evaluation project was undertaken.

WHAT IS BEING EVALUATED?

What was sought in the evaluation? The first concern was with changes that are taking place in teachers and children as a result of the community study experiences. Specifically, it was sought to learn: (1) How the program has affected the participant's attitudes toward students, toward fellow-teachers, toward parents, and toward other people in the community, (2) how it has influenced methods of teaching and content of subject-matter and curriculum design with regard to school-community relations, (3) how it has changed the participant's attitudes toward the community in which he teaches and toward the city as a whole, and (4) what effect the program has had upon the civic attitude of participants in terms of their willingness to give personal time and energy to worthy community causes.

The second concern was with the program itself. What factors—trips, meetings, discussions—in the program were especially effective in creating the desirable changes? Specifically: (1) which activities in the first-, second- and third-year programs and in the seminar were particularly valuable experiences, (2) which activities had little or doubtful effect on the creation of desirable changes in teachers and in the environment, (3) which experiences had negative effects and might well be eliminated from the program, (4) what changes might be made in current practices, and (5) what new experiences might be incorporated into the program.

THE TECHNIQUES USED

The data used in the evaluation fell into three categories; first, questionnaire data submitted by 546 respondents; second, 300 samplings from teachers' recordings handed in by participants at the close of each first-year's program; third, reports of significant changes motivated by community study and having an ongoing and widespread relationship with curriculum design and with improved school-community relationships.

THE QUESTIONNAIRE DATA

Questionnaire responses were submitted by 546 of the participants in the program during the year 1950-51. This number does not represent all those who were in the program that year, but it does include about 80 per cent of all those currently participating. Moreover, it represents every level of participation—first-, second-, third-year programs and the seminar.

The questionnaire dealt with activities undertaken in each level of the program from the first year through the seminar. Respondents submitted reactions to the community study experiences which they had had in past years, as well as during the year 1950-51. Thus, for example, seminar respondents submitted data on their three previous years of participation as well as on their current program.

An effort was made to discover the extent to which the first-year experiences were the first-time community contacts of the participants in the religious, cultural, and interracial areas. The questions and responses are given below:

FIRST-TIME CONTACT WITH CHURCHES

1. Which of these churches had you not visited for a service or an explanation of religious culture patterns before taking the community study?

No. of Teachers

a. Roman Catholic Church 142
   (30.6 per cent of the 464 non-Roman
   Catholics)
b. Jewish Synagogue or Temple 361
   (76.6 per cent of 471 non-Jews)
c. Greek Orthodox 464
   (86.0 per cent of 539 non-Greek Orthodox)
d. Protestant Church 58
   (39.7 per cent of 146 non-Protestants)

2. Which of these interracial contacts did you not have before
taking community study?

No. of Teachers

   a. Visit to Morgan College or Madison Avenue
YWCA 465
     (94.1 per cent of 494 white teachers) *

   b. Lecture on bi-racial relations as a Negro
sees it 395
     (79.9 per cent of 494 white teachers)

  * Teachers were asked to note their schools by number and
thus number of white respondents were identified.

FIRST-TIME CONTACTS WITH HOUSING EXPERIENCES

The desire here was to find out to what extent trips to
the slums and to public-housing projects were first-time experiences for participants. The same ideas were in mind in
connection with the housing lectures noted. The degree to
which these housing experiences were new is pointed out
by the responses noted below.

1. Which of these housing experiences had you not participated
in before taking community study?

No. of Teachers

   a. Conducted tours of slums 491
     (89.9 per cent of total group)

   b. Visit to public housing project 398
     (72.8 per cent of total group)

   c. Observation of films and slides on housing
problems in Baltimore 385
     (70.5 per cent of total group)

   d. Lecture on housing, by authorities 386
     (70.6 per cent of total group)

FIRST-TIME CONTACTS WITH SELECTED
GOVERNMENT EXPERIENCES

The data below indicate that large numbers of Baltimore teachers had few experiences with government before taking the community study. This is particularly true when it comes to understanding county government, though it also holds for city government since few had ever been in the Board of Estimates Room or City Council Chamber at the Baltimore City Hall. Surprisingly enough, over 28 per cent had never been in the City Hall Building.

1. Which of these governmental experiences had you not participated in before taking community study?

No. of Teachers

a. Visit to Baltimore County Court House ... 401
   (73.2 per cent of the total group)

b. First-hand explanations by officials in county government 466
   (85.3 per cent of the total group)

c. Visit to Baltimore City Hall 158
   (28.9 per cent of the total group)

d. Visit to Board of Estimates Room or City Council Chamber 422
   (77.2 per cent of the total group)

e. First-hand explanation by officials in city government 420
   (76.9 per cent of the total group)

Use of Community Study Experiences

The aim here was to find out how community study experiences were affecting (1) teaching relationships with students, (2) relationships with faculty members and parents, (3) relationships with community agencies and (4) voluntary community services on the part of participants.

The table that follows includes tabulations for various kinds of applications of community study. Except for field trips, the percentages go up with the levels of participation and are particularly high for the seminar group.

PERCENTAGE OF TEACHERS APPLYING COMMUNITY STUDY
EXPERIENCES ACCORDING TO LEVEL OF PARTICIPATION
(in round numbers)

| TYPES OF APPLICATION | LEVEL OF PARTICIPATION | | | | | | |
	1st Year % *	1st-2nd Year %	2nd Year %	3rd Year %	Seminar %	All Years Number	%
Teachers taking field trips with own students this year, stimulated by community study.	65	51	46	48	41	281	51
Teachers promoting plays, projects, and other activities, stimulated by community study.	39	42	44	45	82	243	46
Teachers having contacts with faculty members and PTA, stimulated by community study.	46	50	54	54	82	293	54
Teachers having contacts with community agencies, stimulated by community study.	18	20	31	42	73	171	31
Teachers doing occasional civic voluntary work outside school, stimulated by community study.	15	16	18	22	91	106	20
Teachers doing continuing voluntary work outside school, stimulated by community study.	9	6	9	13	54	64	12

* Per cent in each case is based on number of respondents in that category: 1st year, 124; 1st and 2nd years together, 86; 2nd year, 158; 3rd year, 156; seminar, 22.

SAMPLINGS FROM PARTICIPANTS' RECORDINGS

At the end of each year, first-year participants were asked to submit a paper indicating the implications of their community study experiences for their own teaching situations or for their responsibilities as citizens in Baltimore.

Since June, 1947, when the first group completed the first-year program, about a thousand such papers have been turned in. Around half of these reports include unsolicited responses indicating personal reactions to the program and mention specific educational changes which have resulted from participation. These unsolicited responses are in record form and include enough detail to make them very useful for evaluation purposes.

Approximately 300 of the 1000 papers turned in by first-year participants were examined. The technique used was to select a sampling of about a third of the papers from each year's group from 1947 through 1950. These 300 papers were read for the purpose of discovering unsolicited responses indicating changes in teachers' attitudes, teaching methods, subject-matter content, and curriculum design.

CHANGES IN TEACHERS' ATTITUDES AND UNDERSTANDINGS ABOUT BALTIMORE

On the whole, teachers indicated that the community study program made them more alert to the city's problems, shocked them about some situations, and developed for them a deeper understanding of the relationships between the environment and what and how students learn. Teachers new to Baltimore were especially vocal about the need for such experiences, but a number of the natives felt they had not really known the city.

CHANGES IN TEACHERS' OWN ATTITUDES TOWARD PEOPLE OF OTHER CULTURES

The participants' records show that the culture-pattern series had a profound effect on changing the attitudes of teachers toward people of other religious faiths and other races. For example, for a number of teachers, the Eutaw Place Temple meeting marked the first contact with a Jewish religious service. This meeting helped break down stereotypes which had been held for years. The meetings at the Roman Catholic Cathedral and at Morgan College were often indicated as "first contacts" with Roman Catholics and Negroes, and the beginnings of new appreciations and understandings. A few teachers commented about "improved understandings about the Christian Science Church." An interesting comment was made by one participant who said, "I feel stronger in my own faith but more understanding and appreciative of others' faiths and their right to worship freely."

CHANGES IN TEACHERS' ATTITUDES TOWARD CHILDREN OF OTHER CULTURES

The participants' records were particularly encouraging in this area of teacher-pupils relations. As one teacher put it, "Now I know why it is so important for Hebrew children not to be detained and kept from their afternoon religious schools." Another teacher talked about the new regard in which she was held by her Greek pupil who knew about her visit to the Greek church. Yet another teacher indicated a more sympathetic attitude toward Roman Catholic pupils who asked to be excused from school in order to attend religious retreats. Teachers seemed to be seeing many more events through the eyes of the students.

CHANGES IN TEACHERS' ATTITUDES TOWARD
BALTIMORE'S HOUSING PROBLEMS

The participants' records show that teachers were "impressed," "shocked," "amazed," "aroused," and "ready to do something" about Baltimore's housing situation. While teachers new to Baltimore seemed more disturbed about their first-hand contacts with the slum problems, many natives indicated that they had been totally unaware of the situation. Moreover, these new attitudes stimulated definite action on the part of teachers so aroused. Action programs, so stimulated, are recorded elsewhere in this report and serve as further evidence of changes in attitudes.

CHANGES IN TEACHERS' ATTITUDES TOWARD
CHILDREN FACING HOUSING PROBLEMS

Perhaps the most responses in this area were by those who "saw children's dirty faces in an entirely new light." A number of teachers commented on the need for understanding difficult home situations. Perhaps the most understanding comment was by the teacher who said, "Now that I have seen an outside toilet that serves 37 people, I know why Jane has a good reason for asking permission to go to the lavatory the first hour every day." The most homespun comment was made by the teacher who said, "The home environment for these boys and girls is so cold and drab, my classroom must be warm and colorful."

CHANGES IN TEACHING PRACTICES ABOUT HOUSING

Classroom activities in art, industrial arts, music, English, and social studies were indicative of some of the ways in which the first-year community study experiences were affecting teaching practice. The most effective activities were those which used the school's own housing problems as a jumping-off point for extended studies in this area.

While these changes in teaching practices were not as dramatic as those made by participants in the second- and third-year groups, they nevertheless showed that the teachers wanted to do something after being aroused about the housing problem.

CHANGES IN TEACHING PRACTICES ABOUT INTERGROUP RELATIONS

The participants' records noted show that teachers were anxious to have their pupils appreciate and understand the religious beliefs of their fellow classmates. Plays, pageants, trips, speakers, and projects helped bring about these desired understandings. Perhaps most important of all were the efforts of teachers to bring together children of different backgrounds in order to work co-operatively on problems not necessarily intercultural in nature.

A few teachers were doing something about better race relationships. Some were bringing Negro and white children together on co-operative programs.

CHANGES IN TEACHING PRACTICES ABOUT GOVERNMENT

Few participants seemed to be doing significant work dealing with improved understanding of government. Perhaps they were doing more than they reported. It may be that because the government meetings were not so impressive as the others, there was also less follow-up. The participants' records show that where classroom practice was changing, it seemed to be a result of follow-up of field trip procedures demonstrated in the workshop.

Significant Ongoing Changes

In addition to the questionnaire data and the participants' records, a number of published reports indicate that the community study program has brought about improved curriculum design, more functional classroom procedures, and better community living. For example, in two high schools the modern problems course was changed basically to provide for civic experience by students. School facilities have been opened to the public at a junior high school. A scrap-iron junk yard opposite a school was cleaned up after two years of community help, and transformed into a new recreation field. In a junior high school an experimental parent-adolescent weekly social program has been developed. In three schools in an underprivileged area, an important pilot housing improvement project is under way. In all cases such programs as these have been the result, in part or in full, of participation in community study.

PERSPECTIVE

Several evaluative criteria of real significance are implicit in each of the accounts here presented. First is the basic premise that the objectives of the program are the criteria for its appraisal. Sometimes the purposes are clearly identified at the very beginning—as in Norristown, where a survey of the physical needs of the community, and a listing of the conditions needing improvement were the first step in the new program. Moreover, the goals were made specific. To discover problems and to do something about them is another way of establishing goals—the first step in evaluation as it is in the solution of problems. The two steps, in fact, are implicit each in the other.

One of the first moves taken in the Norristown community was a survey of needs and a listing of the conditions which needed remedy. Evaluation thus began here. It was extended further, however, by the questions raised about how the situations revealed by the survey could be met. These were, in a sense, descriptive of procedures and definitions of the job. While these or similar procedures are essential, they suggest also an important principle in evaluation.

The goals of Ascension Parish Project were also specific. The over-all goals were those of the improvement of living through community education. This is a large order, and so the general purpose was broken down into smaller and more specific objectives. These were: (1) to improve rural life in all of its phases; (2) to develop fully the natural and human resources of the community; (3) to improve health—especially nutrition, sight, speech, and oral hygiene; (4) to improve housing and sanitation; (5) to increase co-operation among schools, homes, agencies and communities; (6) to establish a Parish library; and (7) to interpret activities and programs to the public. These more specific objectives were again narrowed for immediate emphasis to three aspects: (1) nutrition; (2) the health of school children—especially as to teeth and eyes; and (3) a live-at-home farm production program.

These objectives had the advantage of being strengthened by the common agreement of many people—in fact, by all those who were to participate in the program. These included the Parish Superintendent of Schools and his Board; the Extension Service; the Parish Health Unit, the Parish Department of Public Welfare; the Veterans Farm Training Supervisor; the Production and Marketing Administration, representatives from clubs, churches, and citizens groups; the State Department of Education; the State Department of Health; the State Department of Public

Welfare; the Louisiana State University and Experiment Station; the General Education Board; and other agencies.

Baltimore's major aims—child acculturation, curriculum revision, and community action—were likewise identified as such after the first community study project was under way. In Floodwood, by contrast, the objectives were not specifically preconceived; rather they were widely generalized in terms of "raising the level of living of the people in the community." This broad purpose was later made specific as the program itself developed in many directions. Baltimore's aims became more comprehensive than either Norristown's or Ascension Parish's. In all of the reports, however, the basic principle of appraising the program directly in terms of the objectives sought was observed. If health improvement is the goal of a project then the improvement of health is the real test, not health knowledge, nor even health habits. If a major aim is widespread teacher participation in civic action, then evaluation must be made in terms of both the quantity and the quality of such participation.

Secondly, if we may judge from the reports, it is good practice in community evaluation to use as many techniques as possible. From the earliest stages of any program, careful systematic evaluation should be made and adequate records kept. Simple appraisal methods as well as scientific instruments should be used. Evaluation is not esoteric, nor is it always involved. It is a common experience, for example, to see improvement in programs taking place and human beings taking delight in it. The people of Norristown, for example, must have felt considerable pride in seeing order emerge from disorder, neatness from disarray and beauty where before there had been ugliness. Evaluation then, is a human problem as well as one of figures, graphs and questionnaires.

The application of measuring instruments such as the
Ohio Teaching Record used in the Norristown school and
the standardized tests at Floodwood is an important phase
of evaluation. Observations, even under controlled conditions, are likely to be colored by the type of person who
observes and while actual figures are more reliable they
tell only part of a story. Whenever possible, it does seem
wise to use a commonly-accepted instrument, tested by experience, to measure progress. The standardized instrument itself frequently begets confidence in the results of
the study, and its use should not be overlooked in an evaluative program. Baltimore, for example, used many types of
formal devices in the evaluation of its program. Questionnaires, also employed by Norristown, anecdotal records,
surveys to measure change in curriculum and method, and
the amount of civic participation by teachers enrolled in
successive stages of the three-year cycle were also used.

The use of informal ways of evaluation was reported also
in many of the reports. The mass meeting of the people in
the Norristown community was one such. Held at the end
of the school year, the meeting provided a realistic method
of deciding how much had been accomplished in meeting
the goals established early in the school year and with
what quality of performance the goals had been met. A face-
to-face technique of talking things over is an excellent
method of appraisal. Evaluation thus becomes not only a
summing-up process, but a creative one as well. Discussions
of progress and its results are not only good for people but
they are, in truth, two of the ways by which democracy
works.

The consideration by the Floodwood School of basic community factors is another informal but important phase of
evaluation. The pioneer traditions, the in-and-out groups,
the pressures of the timber and mercantile interests, the

local development of co-operatives and teachers' union affected the results of community efforts and the Floodwood community was wise to recognize the fact. Such factors may be major items in the evaluation of a community program and unless they are known and understood, community development may be retarded or even made impossible. Other informal methods of evaluation in the Floodwood report were illustrated by the use the opinions of teachers and children in the evaluation of school programs, reports to the local Board of Education, student polls, conferences with parents, and so on.

The third evaluative principle apparent in all four accounts is the emphasis placed upon self-appraisal by the groups. Both insight and interest are most likely to develop in a community program when all share in diagnosing its effectiveness. The rural community at Norristown, as stated above, staged a mass meeting in which the lay people as well as the teachers made down-to-earth appraisals of the extent to which their goals had been achieved, and the quality present in their achievement. Workshop groups in the Baltimore study, through evaluation of the program, assisted planning committees to move forward. Floodwood secured program appraisals from students, parents, and other lay people, as well as from the teachers and administrators. Evaluation in Ascension Parish operated through the team concept of appraisal, but here was stressed also the evaluation by officials from community agencies, and actual record keeping by children, parents, and teachers. Regardless of the use of specific procedures, however, the widespread sharing of evaluation by many people apparently provides the "self-analysis quality" considered essential for continued interest, and effective action.

Fourth, it appears that the simple matter of keeping records is as important in the evaluation of a community proj-

ect as it is in other research studies. The assembling of
evidence is important, but the result must be recorded if it
is to be used. Records in terms of actual figures are important, too, as the Norristown report indicates. These reflect
trends, and most evaluative procedures depend upon them
for telling at least a part of the story. Records of membership and attendance in such organizations as the Parent-
Teachers Association and the Farm and Home Bureaus are
valuable data, frequently not kept. In a very important way
such records act as a barometer indicating whether interest
is high or low, ephemeral or consistent. The increase in
memberships and attendance in the community organizations of Norristown had real significance, because they
indicate that the programs in progress were vital and significant to people in general. This constitutes a real test of
a program.

The Ascension Parish report well exemplifies the importance of keeping records. The assembling of evidence in
this evaluation program was undertaken by the use of acceptable techniques. Moreover, the sources of the data were
defensible. These included the annual reports of various
parish agencies active in the plan, and interviews with the
agency workers, as well as many rural people. Meetings
were held in different sections of the Parish where opinions
were expressed, pooled and recorded. Field trips were made
and the results tabulated. School rooms and lunchrooms
were visited and information secured through personal
interviews.

Surveys both preceding and following the nutritional
program were instituted and careful records were kept.
Record-keeping was made a part of an educational process
in which parents, children, and teachers participated. This
joint participation in the research project gave it according
to the report "a quality which is highly desirable for its

own sake and for motivating value; it set the stage for action."

Evidences of the changes taking place in children and in the community were carefully assembled over a two-year period, and were tabulated and recorded. Data for the changes taking place in diets were secured from the nutritional surveys, and by observation of the value placed on school lunches. Data on the community changes in diet were assembled from personal interviews with parents, school board members and citizens of all types. Records were kept also on the number of increased calls made by the citizens in the Parish on home economics teachers and home demonstration agents, on the assumption that an increase in requests for assistance indicated a corresponding increase in interest. Data were also gathered on the increase in the number of home gardens, and the installation of a canning center to take care of the agricultural surpluses. Children reported improvements at home to their teachers and records were kept.

As the school curriculum became more functional, records were made of the changes. Correlation of subject matter with community-school programs became the order of the day. Spelling, writing, arithmetic, and geography were used to serve the community-school goals. Science, art, agriculture and home economics also made their contributions. The reporting on this feature is valuable not only because it points up the desirability of class instruction being tied closely with community interests, but it provides desirable clues on how this can be accomplished.

Finally, as the reports indicate, a good evaluation program reveals frequently the concomitant results of a community program, and these may well be more important than the original goals. The development of new interests and leadership in the communities was evident in all of the reports. Demonstration that co-operative efforts pay, and that they pay large dividends, was also reported. The lifting of the sights of those at the grass roots was an inspiring part of all the records. These results are in many ways incidental to the major objectives but they deserve evaluation at regular intervals. In a very real sense, however, the incidental achievements of community projects are in the periphery of progress, and they also point the way to future programs.

Educating for
Dynamic Democracy

Parts I and II have portrayed activities which the committee has considered representative of the community school. Some of those accounts represent in the fullness described extensions of anything that now exists, but at any particular point they are not far ahead of current best practice somewhere. They are achievable in the schools of today. The purpose of this section is to help analyze our present educational setting to see if we can make it possible for more schools to move rapidly in the directions indicated. All of us share a feeling of great urgency to achieve an education adequate for our democracy in a world of conflict. We seek help in improving our practices toward such ends.

The concern of this section, then, is to set forth the factors which will help us make our schools "community schools" in the best possible sense. We are concerned about the question of "how," although we approach this question from the standpoint of basic principles and not in terms of detailed practices. That is why we now sketch the essence of community-school thinking, and then indicate certain sociological, psychological, and educational factors which together provide valid foundation for needed advances toward actual achievement of the community school ideal.

6

The Community School Concept

W‌E SHOULD LIKE FIRST TO reaffirm our concern for values. We believe that means and ends are inseparable. The community school cannot be built in just any community, no matter how skillful the board of education members and the professional educators may be. Only in those communities where there is full respect for human personality, where shared judgments are valued and sought, where the highest gains are those which bring better relations between all persons, will there be the kind of freedom that is necessary to develop the interrelationship of school and community described in previous sections.

RECENT DEVELOPMENTS

If this were a documentary film we would at this point show "flash backs" to previous sections and thus highlight the community school's chief characteristics already described. As we now quote from previous sections of this book we ask our readers to remember the spirit of the situations there presented.

The improvement of the quality of human living, both personal and social, became accepted as the function of education.

The schools now serve the community and the community is part of the "school."

Buildings, grounds, equipment, recreation facilities and the personnel of the schools are made available to any group which is helping further the well-being of our people.

In the larger sense, all citizens have educational functions to perform and therefore may be thought of as teachers.

The democratic test of leadership is in the number and variety of leaders.

Instruction is informal always, but it is not haphazard.

The school in co-operation with the Community Council helps the people identify and analyze community problems.

Visitors to Visby are confused by the absence of many of the attributes of "school" that they have unconsciously presumed to be indispensable.

Those descriptions of ideal and actual situations now need to be further analyzed for their unique aspects which make them different from good education generally. Certainly there are many emphases in the above selections which have always characterized the work of sensitive educators.

Descriptive labels have value when they help us differentiate aspects previously dimly seen, if at all. To state that "the major purpose of the community school is the life-long preparation of all persons for effective social living" is an important reaffirmation of a great faith—but it gives us little clue as to the respects in which community education is different from the centuries of good educational practice which have helped to develop better citizens.

An earlier section of this report has pointed out that the school, in one sense, is always a community school. No school can exist without some relations to the society which makes it possible. The term "community school" as used here, however, refers to a specific development in American education in recent years, and it is this development to which we address ourselves. Out of many writings of the past twenty years we present a few which are representative of the ways in which educators today are thinking about the community school.

1938

A notable bench mark in the development of the community school concept was the Society for Curriculum Study's volume, *The Community School.*[1] Edited by Samuel Everett, this was the first book to deal comprehensively with the community school as such. In it were presented nine philosophic issues which were felt to be involved in the kind of education represented by the community school:

1. All life is education *vs.* education is gained only in formal institutions of learning.
2. Education requires participation *vs.* education is adequately gained through studying about life.
3. Adults and children have fundamental common purposes in both work and play *vs.* adults are primarily concerned with work and children with play.
4. Public school systems should be primarily concerned with the improvement of community living and improvement of the social order *vs.* school systems should be primarily concerned with passing on the cultural heritage.
5. The curriculum should receive its social orientation from major problems *vs.* the curriculum oriented in relation to specialized aims of academic subjects.
6. Public education should be founded upon democratic processes and ideal *vs.* the belief that most children and most adults are incapable of intelligently running their own lives or participating in common group efforts.
7. Progress in education and in community living best comes through the development of common concerns among individuals and social groups *vs.* progress best comes through development of clear-cut social classes and vested interest groups which struggle for survival and dominance.

[1] New York: D. Appleton-Century Company, 1938.

8. Public schools should be responsible for the education of both children and adults *vs.* public schools should only be responsible for the education of children.

9. Teacher-preparatory institutions should prepare youth and adults to carry on a community type of public education *vs.* such institutions should prepare youth and adults to perpetuate academic traditions and practices.

These issues, it was emphasized, were to be tested by the nature and extent of various kinds of experiences characterizing schools, and not by the assertions of the persons in charge. For example, most school personnel would verbally agree with the idea in (1) that educational experiences are found among all the activities in which an individual is involved, but would actually proceed to develop the program of their schools with very little reference to the educational experiences students have outside of school.

1941

Lloyd Allen Cook suggested that

any school is a community school to the extent that it seeks to realize some such objectives as the following: (a) educates youth by and for participation in the full range of basic life activities (human needs, areas of living, persistent problems, etc.); (b) seeks increasingly to democratize life in school and outside; (c) uses community resources in all aspects of its program; (d) actively co-operates with other social agencies and groups in improving community life; (e) functions as a service center for youth and adult groups.[2]

[2] "School and Community" in *Encyclopedia of Educational Research*, first edition, page 1002 (New York: Macmillan, 1941).

1945

In their *School and Community*, Edward G. Olsen and others identified six basic principles around which the community school operates.[3] Such a school:

1. Evolves purposes out of the interests and needs of people.
2. Utilizes a wide variety of community resources in its program.
3. Practices and promotes democracy in all activities of school and community.
4. Builds the curriculum around the major processes and problems of human living.
5. Exercises definite leadership for the planned and co-operative improvement of group living in community and larger areas.
6. Enlists children and adults in co-operative group projects of common interest and mutual concern.

In the *Forty-fourth Yearbook* of the National Society for the Study of Education, Maurice F. Seay defined the community school as one which maintains

> two distinctive emphases—service to the entire community, not merely to the children of school age; and discovery, development, and use of the resources of the community as part of the educational facilities of the school. The concern of the community school with the local community is intended, not to restrict the school's attention to local matters, but to provide a focus from which to relate study and action in the larger community—the state, the region, the nation, the world.[4]

[3] New York: Prentice-Hall, 1945, p. 11.
[4] "The Community-School Emphases in Postwar Education." National Society for the Study of Education, *American Education in the Postwar Period*, Part I: *Curriculum Reconstruction*, Chapter X (Chicago: University of Chicago Press, 1945).

He presented also six principles which should guide the development of a community educational program:

1. Since education is a continuous process, it cannot be confined within fixed administrative divisions; but for education to be most effective there must be co-ordination of all educational services in a community.

2. When educational activities are based upon the needs and interests of those for whom they are planned, community problems assume primary importance in the school's curriculum, and the school utilizes the community's resources in the solution of community problems.

3. The democratic method in education is a practicable method to use in an educational program based on community problems and interests.

4. An educational program designed for all age levels of a community is characterized by flexibility—space and equipment serve multiple purposes; the materials of instruction are adaptable and the methods pliable; requirements for attendance and credit are adjustable.

5. The teacher in a community school is a member of the community.

6. A community school makes its physical plant and environment a community center and a demonstration of desirable operation and maintenance of property.

1947

Guiding principles which serve to give direction to the many activities which are the proper function of a community school are outlined in the ASCD Yearbook, *Organizing the Elementary School for Living and Learning:* [5]

1. The staff understand and appreciate the reciprocal relationship which exists between the school and its supporting community.

2. The school explores the community, discovers its needs and

[5] Washington: Association for Supervision and Curriculum Development of the National Education Association, 1947. pp. 78-118.

problems, and utilizes its resources to work toward a solution of these problems.

3. The organization of the school provides for co-operative planning of a school-community program.
4. The community builds a school that serves all its people.
5. The school evaluates its program by criteria of good school-community living.

William K. McCharan in 1947 defined the community school in his *Selected Community School Programs in the South* as "one that has developed a program of activities designed for effective and useful learning on the part of children and which helps to improve community living; one which serves the total population of the community and seeks to evolve its purpose out of the interests and needs of the people living in the community." [6] Some characteristics of practice in such schools were:

1. The administrative policy includes democratic participation, public services started and operated by the school, co-operative group projects of children and adults on common interests and concerns, services available to the total population, and surveys to discover and base programs on needs, interests, and resources of the community.
2. Instruction uses community resources, problems of living, provides work experience, creative activities, is based on children's needs. There is a definite program to improve instruction.
3. The school stimulates home improvement, raises the standards of living, gives children a chance to take part in community programs, and co-operates with other organizations and agencies.
4. The community participates with the school in solving community problems, provides and uses school facilities for the whole year, co-operates in planning the educational program, needs continuity in leadership.

[6] Nashville: George Peabody College for Teachers, 1948. See his Chapter II, "The Community Concept of Education"; also Chapters IV, V, VI and VII.

5. The teachers live in the community, organize an in-service program, have deep convictions, are concerned with child welfare, work with many individuals and agencies, enrich textbook materials.

6. The children are responsible for useful tasks at school, learn things through discovering them for themselves, share in planning the program, live and work co-operatively, learn of the community's potential as a home, have access to vocational courses, economic experiences, help protect school property, engage in student government, develop leadership in clubs and committees.

Milosh Muntyan analyzed community school concepts as revealed in the professional literature to 1947.[7] He found two basic approaches in the concept:

1. To bring various activities of community life into the school, making of these activities the heart of the school program.

2. To take the school out into the community, centering the school program around their activities, as they operate in the community situation.

Both of these approaches, however, commonly have internal points of emphasis which should be recognized since they represent actually the real purposes of these divergent conceptions of the community school. Specifically, both these approaches to the problem of integrating school and community can have three distinct points of emphasis. First, the community can be brought into the school, or the school can be taken out into the community, primarily for school purposes, i.e. simply to facilitate the usual "school learnings" through the use of various aspects of the community as "subject matter."

Second, the purpose can be primarily community centered, i.e. to make social service agents of the school and

[7] *Community School Concepts in Relation to Societal Determinants.* Urbana, Illinois: University of Illinois, 1947. Summarized in the *Journal of Educational Research* 41:597-609; April, 1948.

the school population, without any particular interest in the educational aspects of such service.

Third, the purpose can be school-community centered, i.e., making a service agency of the school and its population even while the community is used as the "subject matter" of the school's program.

1948

The National Conference of Professors of Educational Administration agreed that "the basic method and purpose of education must become that of improving the quality of daily living in communities." Sixteen characteristics of the community school were listed: [8]

1. The community school seeks to operate continuously as an important unit in the family of agencies serving the common purpose of improving community living.
2. The community school shares with citizens continuing responsibility for the identification of community needs and the development of subsequent action programs to meet these needs.
3. The community school begins its responsibility for better living with the immediate school environment.
4. The curriculum of the community school is sufficiently comprehensive and flexible to facilitate the realization of its purpose.
5. The community school program is dynamic, constantly changing to meet emerging community needs.
6. The community school makes full use of all community resources for learning experiences.
7. The community school develops and uses distinctive types of teaching materials.
8. The community school shares with other agencies the responsibility for providing opportunities for appropriate learning experiences for all members of the community.

[8] See John Lund, "Education Can Change Community Life." *School Life* 31:11-12; November, 1948.

9. The community school recognizes improvement in social and community relations behavior as an indication of individual growth and development.

10. The community school develops continuous evaluation in terms of the quality of living for pupils, teachers, and administrators; for the total school program; and for the community.

11. The pupil personnel services of the community school are co-operatively developed in relation to community needs.

12. The community school secures staff personnel properly prepared to contribute to the distinctive objectives of the school, facilitates effective work and continuous professional growth by members of the staff, and maintains only those personnel policies which are consistent with the school's purposes.

13. The community school maintains democratic pupil-teacher-administrator relationships.

14. The community school creates, and operates in, a situation where there is high expectancy of what good schools can do to improve community living.

15. The community school buildings, equipment, and grounds are so designed, constructed, and used as to make it possible to provide for children, youth, and adults, those experiences in community living which are not adequately provided by agencies other than the school.

16. The community school budget is the financial plan for translating into reality the educational program which the school board, staff members, students, and other citizens have agreed upon as desirable for the community.

1950

In further refinement of earlier writings, Cook suggested that the community school is not

something different and apart from public education. On the contrary, the idea represents a trend in modern schooling, a direction in which some schools everywhere are moving. . . . Judging chiefly from work over the years in such schools, any school can be called a community school to the extent that it operates along somewhat the following lines: [9]

1. Regards education as a lifelong process, rather than in terms of present school-age years, available to every citizen at public costs.
2. Conceives its basic function as meeting the life-needs of learners, with need defined in reference to democratic values and growth potentials.
3. Educates youth by providing experiences in the full range of life-activities, stressing especially the use of intelligence and group action in problem solving.
4. Conducts the school as a functional community, a democratic system of human relations in which every participant is valued and treated in terms of personal worth.
5. Views the teacher as a manager of the group learning process, exhibiting the kinds of group work and technical skills which this implies.
6. Makes the local community an object of special study accepting as the chief measure of the school's worth its ability to improve the area's way of living.
7. Uses local community resources to educate for life at home and "abroad," ever conscious of our increasingly complex and interdependent world.
8. Serves as a community center for youth and adult groups and co-operates actively with agencies interested in the care and well-being of young people.
9. Develops scientific and systematic appraisals of its work as seen in changes in learners, in home living, community conditions, and agency services.

1954

Seven basic characteristics of the community school are described in the revised edition of *School and Community* by Olsen and others, to be published early in 1954.[10] In terms of this listing, the community school:

[9] Lloyd Allen Cook, *A Sociological Approach to Education*, pp. 272-273. New York: McGraw-Hill Book Company, 1950.

[10] Edward G. Olsen and others, *School and Community*, Chapter 1. New York: Prentice-Hall, Inc., 1954.

1. Improves the quality of living here and now.
2. Uses the community as a laboratory for learning.
3. Makes the school plant a community center.
4. Organizes the curriculum around the fundamental processes and problems of living.
5. Includes lay people in school policy and program planning.
6. Leads in community coordination.
7. Practices and promotes democracy in all human relationships.

Although one or more of these seven characteristics may be found in many conventional schools, it is only the Community School which is sufficiently functional and versatile to incorporate them all in balanced manner. This it does because its supporters realize that education is basically a social process; that educational forms and functions must respond to the changing needs of human beings; that democratic education must be able as well as willing to honor its fundamental obligation of helping people to live more effectively and happily, both as individuals and as members of interdependent social groups.

SUMMARY

All these and other notable writings on the community school tend to make it an all-embracing concept. Starting with the relatively simple notion of combining the efforts of school and community for the service and nurture of the child as well as for the improvement of the level of living for the total community, the community-school idea has come to include the most promising ideas and practices in education. The needs-centered curriculum, co-operative planning, interpersonal relations, group processes, problem-solving, world citizenship—all are part of the community-school concept now. One early emphasis which seems to have gone is the matter of improving the social order. Apparently practical projects to make life better for members of the community in such areas as health, food, shelter, recreation, race relations and international understanding are being accomplished without labeling them as attempts to bring about a new social order. Thus we see in these community school summaries the big questions with which education has struggled and will continue to struggle.

Careful evaluation of community school practices indicates that most of them, in one way or another, fall into what may be thought of as four qualitative levels of operation. These levels we now sketch briefly.[11]

The first level includes efforts to make the school itself into an ideal democratic community. To achieve a true democracy all people within the school must co-operate to achieve it. This means administrators, teachers, the school plant maintenance force, and the children. Achievement in democratic living is earned the hard way, through the experience of many people seriously concerned about human relations. Many schools in the United States have begun this concern for human relations in individual classrooms where there are teachers interested in students as people. These classrooms so frequently lead the way to the acceptance of the concept of a community-within-the-school that the process almost becomes a pattern. Here are the teachers who envision children as citizens within a democratic community, and the practices adopted are highly contagious, spreading from room to room. More and more administrators hold to a similar point of view. They conceive of democratic relationships existing between administrator and staff, school board and school personnel, and community members. There are those who would assign to the schools on this level the designation "community-centered," yet emphasis on democratic practices in personal relationships is characteristic of all good schools and is not confined to those properly called "community schools."

[11] This level-analysis was written by Kate Wofford.

At the second level teachers and administrators make serious efforts to relate what is learned verbally in school to what goes on in the community. So far as the actual participation of youth in the life of the community is concerned, many schools in the United States can be found on this level. Yet most teachers still place great confidence in subject-matter as a means of education. When teachers move forward, even a little, from the position that all knowledge is found in textbooks, the practice is hopeful. When teachers begin to relate what is found in textbooks to what is happening in the community, further progress is made. This may be a small step, but for many teachers it is an important one, since it is on this level that teachers frequently begin to develop blocks of subject-matter which find their geneses in the community. On the higher levels of the elementary school and in high school, pupils may even study the community itself, or examine some of its problems. This approach, of course, is still academic if it is used only to supplement the usual textbook lessons. In a subject-matter-dominated school, however, even this step is hopeful and full of promise.

A third level is that of bringing objects and people from the community into the school building, and of taking children into the community. Teachers who operate on this level believe that people learn in many different ways and by a wide use of varied instructional experiences and materials. Nearly all such teachers place much emphasis upon the children actually leaving the school building to study personally what is going on about them in the community. These teachers advocate field trips, interviews, surveys, work experiences, service projects and all sorts of other direct experiences with people and with things to supplement the vicarious experiences had only in books. Many school authorities also make intelligent use of the personnel resources found in communities: people possessing special expertness and knowledge are frequently brought to school to work directly with children and youth. Often this level of activity overlaps that just mentioned. As a matter of fact, if the content of the curriculum is developed from the on-going life processes in which people participate, it is almost impossible to separate the learnings in school from those in the community. To secure the facts necessary to answer community questions and problems, the students must go to the people and to the places where the problems are, and where some answers may be found.

A fourth level is the practice of students, teachers, administrators and lay people together attacking community problems in an effort to improve the quality of their common living. All authorities agree that the achievement of this level of participation is always an essential characteristic of the true community school. When educators accept this point of view and act upon it all sorts of functional activities appear in the school program such as landscaping the school grounds, helping people learn how to farm, to can food, to slaughter animals, to beautify their homes, to improve health conditions, to reduce race, religious and other group tensions, and the like. Such activities are diverse in function, but they all have important elements in common. One of these is the direct attack by the school on community problems which are present and pressing for answers. Another is that practical solutions to these problems generally require the co-operative, planned, organized effort of many people in the community and in the school. A third common element is that such real-life activities can deeply involve the civic abilities of young people, and so appeal greatly to them as they accept the challenges of democratic citizenship in an age of crisis.

In statements of principles or characteristics of community schools, continuing concern is shown for making the school itself a democratic community, for determining and serving the needs of learners and community, for co-operating with other community agencies, for using community resources, both material and human; for stress on people as persons, for building the world community, for systematic use of the problem-solving methods in the community setting, for improving the quality of individual and intergroup living. Most fundamentally we see here the problem of the interrelation of education and action. This requires that we examine the present state of our society and the role of education within it. To understand the role of the "community school" we first need to explore "community education."

CURRENT THINKING

A society may be viewed as the ways by which a number of persons interrelate their various activities in order to achieve a life which by and large for the total group is "best possible." Since individuals are born into and grow up in a society and are not generally self-conscious about their values, the statement as given must be used carefully. It is recognized that there are many conflicting values and that most persons will feel some dissatisfactions, often in fundamental ways. Individuals will tend to associate with others having similar values and will place the interests of such subgroups ahead of the welfare of the total group. The activities by which groups and individuals seek to achieve for themselves the maximum of positive values and to oppose or avoid negative values is the dynamic meaning of "society" and sets the stage for "education."

In this setting there will be many situations where individuals and groups endeavor to modify the actions of others. These efforts will be of many kinds. We may use physical force to compel others to do what we want, we may try to trick them into doing it, we may endeavor to persuade them, we may join with them in the search for new ways of achieving what we both want. "Education" is one of the ways by which we modify the actions of others. Obviously it can be used to cover a variety of these actions, depending upon how one chooses to define it.

We use "education" here to mean the deliberate efforts of a group to modify actions in ways which give all individuals concerned opportunities, commensurate with their abilities, to know and share in the purposes and procedures of the modification. "Education" is a form of action but it is a limited, special form and the two terms are not synonymous.

From the standpoint of the individual we need to consider the relation between the terms "learning" and "education." An individual will engage in many acts. As the result of some of these he will change his way of acting. This change in behavior as a result of previous experience, we call "learning." When someone undertakes to select and organize these experiences so as to get certain learnings in preference to others and to make these selected ones more efficient (more quickly acquired, longer retained, more widely applicable) we have "education." The order of terms in order of increasing specificity is *acting, learning, educating*.

If a society is homogeneous in its make up, learning and educating will be very close together. All of society is united in the values desired and the learner is hardly aware of any educational influences since they are such an integral phase of community living. Neither is the society conscious of education as a special function.

In the more complex societies there are wider differences regarding the values to be inculcated. Since each group tends to be eager to insure the continuance of its values, there is a determined effort to insure the learnings relating to these values. This leads to an emphasis upon education, along with other techniques of social change, by the opposing groups and the learner is thereby frequently faced with conflicting learning situations.

Another development in more complex cultures which creates increased concern for education is a larger number of relatively complex skills which are needed by the young. An industrial society needs a much higher level of verbal competence—reading, writing and arithmetic— and this tends to increase the likelihood that society will turn to persons with specialized skills to handle this teaching. In our American society the expansion of the public school, particularly beyond the elementary level, came as we changed from primarily an agricultural to primarily an industrial society. In order to see more sharply the nature of the demands on education, we turn to a brief comparison of American society today with that of a hundred years ago when many of the characteristics of our public school system were laid down.

Changes in the American Scene

We shall not be able here to analyze in detail all of the major changes. We shall illustrate some of the developments in order to show how they have affected both the general action needs of our society and the consequent educational activities.

In 1850 the majority of the American people were living in settings far simpler than those of our times. It is easy for us to oversimplify life in earlier periods and nothing here is meant to indicate that life was simple. The differences are relative but we believe them to be important.

The world of 1850 was still mainly a decentralized world. Discoveries had already opened up much of the globe, but there had not yet developed the intricate interplay of economic forces which characterize our period. Transportation and communication were still limited. For most Americans most of the time, events in other countries were of little significance. Our decisions were made mainly on a local basis and there was considerable independence even from other parts of our own country.

Life centered pretty much in the local community. A century ago agriculture still dominated the way of life. A great variety of activities were centered in the home. Children were aware of much of the total process of living: the foods they ate were produced largely by their own family or by neighbors, the clothes they wore were fashioned by persons they knew from materials with which they were familiar, the chief problems of government were those of their immediate area and of a scope that they could usually grasp; the morals of the area were commonly accepted and commonly enforced. In such a setting the larger tasks of education were handled outside the school. The work of the school was centered around reading where the facilities of the home and the available time and skill of the elders did not make for sure instruction. At the higher levels the schools were almost entirely designed for youth planning to go into the professions, where again skill in reading was the basic need. The practical side could still be handled by a kind of apprentice arrangement.

In a hundred years changes already impending in 1850

became widespread. The community was no longer the consistent, persistent educating force. Specialization had splintered the integrity of living—splintered it so extensively that many persons at all ages found it difficult to reassemble enough pieces to build a stable mooring. Darwin and the natural sciences had created more questions regarding long-held values than religion and the social sciences could answer. The influx of peoples with different customs complicated the value systems still further. The employment of fathers and sometimes of older siblings and even of mothers reduced the education which the families could provide. The growth of larger and larger urban centers created an anonymity which weakened the educational force of the neighborhood. More and more people looked to the school for help in areas which previously had been the responsibility of the family and the community generally.

The school responded in the way in which it was skilled —through materials which could be *read*. The new demands came at such a terrific rate that there was little time to take a long look—to see if there were other ways to meet new needs. A few persons—for example, John Dewey wrote *School and Society* in 1899—sensed the inadequacies of traditional approaches and suggested ways of broadening the educational experience. Occasional schools here and there tried modifications of the customary pattern. The best work tended to be in the rural areas where the combination of meager resources of verbal materials and the greater readiness of the community made possible a co-operation which suggested the outlines of the "community school." But, in general, the increasing mobility added more and more weight to the modal pattern by penalizing the atypical. It was a rare situation where lay and professional opinion combined to support activities which seemed not to fit the "standard" pattern.

At the very time that the community was putting increased responsibilities on the school to help meet some of the problems created by the decline of the effectiveness of the family and the neighborhood, it was also searching in other directions for new patterns of action. When the town was the chief unit of living, the face-to-face relations culminating in the town meeting served well to build democratic solutions for the various group matters which needed decision. As the cities grew, there was less opportunity to establish these face-to-face understandings and the number of persons involved became so large that direct participation became less possible. Political reforms were tried—referendum, recall, city manager, proportional representation—but the troubles persisted.

Gradually the efforts turned to ways in which more vitality could be restored to the smaller units. In these members could recapture the sense of personal worth and effectiveness which had given way before the frustration of the impersonal system. For many this was so impersonal that a check in front of a name, which often was only a name, seemed to be the essence of citizenship. A war, a depression, and then another war added incentive.

Over the country a surge of self-help movements began to draw attention. Always indigenous to a pioneer society, this process began to reassert itself. From Virginia came the stories of the *New* Dominion. In New York a State Citizens Council asserted and acted on the belief that "a better America will be built in better communities." In Kentucky, in Michigan, in Montana, in hundreds of places throughout the land, the movement spread. Education was always part of this process—often not very clearly defined but present in the search for persons with skills, particularly of human relations, which would meet the many needs as citizens worked with one another. Adult education, not in the old limited terms but in the broad effort to help adults when they need help, was growing rapidly.

So we find a situation today in which in all areas of action our society is seeking better ways of meeting the demands it faces. In the school, many new developments such as group projects, core curricula, work programs and democratic administration methods illustrate efforts to make the school itself more effective in meeting the growing responsibilities. In the community, co-operative associations, community chests, volunteer offices, community councils illustrate parallel efforts. Thus the community school represented an effort on the part of the school to secure the help of the community; the community development programs included attempts to secure a broad educational base. The healthy community requires pervasive educational services: an effective education requires the vital activities and resources of the whole community as well as the school. Before we examine the possibilities created by the merging of these streams, let us look at developments in the area of resources for the jobs to be done.

7

Developing Your Community School

FINDINGS ABOUT LEARNING

O<small>NE OF THE MOST VALUABLE</small> assets available in considering how to get a more adequate education is research in the field of learning. This work centers in psychology but some of the most important insights have come from psychiatry and anthropology. The major work in psychology has been done in the last fifty years and we are only at the beginning of an adequate science of behavior. The earlier work was strongly influenced by the analytic approach of the physical sciences— the individual tended to be treated as an isolated entity that could be broken down into reaction units. The work of Freud and others in showing the complex interrelations of the emotional aspects of behavior, the work of the social anthropologists in broadening our awareness of the societal context of behavior, and the development of methods appropriate to the school sciences have helped to give us a fuller understanding of the learning process. All of these insights are of crucial importance.

We are concerned here, therefore, with the problem of how learning relates to the way the whole personality develops. The awareness on the part of good teachers, for example, that learning the multiplication table could not be divorced from other aspects of living was one of the things that pushed schools beyond their walls into other community activities.

We do not propose here to try to develop a complete analysis of learning. We shall try to illustrate the kinds of knowledge which are contributing to our thinking in this area of the community school. We shall especially look for the relations between learning and teaching.

Learning, as was stated above, is used here to mean the changing of behavior in some degree of permanence as the result of experience. It thus includes the great bulk of behavior ranging from such things as ways of holding oneself erect (posture) to learning to spell, to learning how to invent the atomic bomb, to beliefs about right and wrong (values). Everyone learns, and everyone learns throughout life. His experiences, which are the basis of his learnings, are found through all his activities—at home, at work, in the church, in the club, in the school. It is this pervasiveness of learning, as we shall show more fully later, that helps to emphasize the place of the whole community in the educational picture.

1. *Everyone learns in order to achieve or make progress toward his goals or values.*

   This does not mean that the learner can always consciously identify the goals toward which he is striving. The work of Freud has helped to make clear the complexity of purposive behavior.

   For an "outsider" (that is, the teacher, anyone planfully working at attempting to change behavior) to say that certain ways of behaving *must be learned* in order to live effectively in modern American society merely means that the person who makes that statement, and possibly others, believes this to be the case. The potential learner may not yet be ready to agree.

   To learn what *must* be learned in order to work efficiently, to act democratically, to communicate with others, to maintain physical and mental health requires that these goals must be valued *by the people who are to do the learning.* Trying to teach good work habits to a boy who does not value good work habits is largely a waste of time. The boy will value good work habits if (a) these habits are perceived by him as contributing to the achievement of his goals and (b) he has a chance to practice them under circumstances that show him that they do so contribute. In this matter of the basis for one's goals, the importance of meaningful groups (where members have positive choice values for one another) is being realized. This is another lead into the total community as educator. An essential element in teaching, therefore, is the creation of learning situations that focus attention on valuation or goal definition and examination. We want an educational program that encourages and helps learners to scrutinize their own values and reflect upon them, reducing inconsistencies, clarifying implications for behavior, and deliberately testing them in action.

This value aspect of learning is continuous and progressive. It must take account of the abilities of the learner, and it must be an integral part of his work and play. It is easy to overdo the abstract and the moral aspects. It is so difficult to know how *the learner* sees it all! This is another illustration of the need to plan sequential opportunities to help each person grow in this respect.

2. *The most basic goals are the deep emotional needs—need to have a sense of belonging, of being wanted, of succeeding.*

The early work in psychology concentrated on the habits and skills which stood out in the learning situations of that time—memorizing, running mazes, telegraphing. Only gradually—Freud deserves much credit at this point—did workers become aware of the fact that attitudes and values were learned, and that personality develops out of the complex of relationships in which the individual lives.

We pointed out earlier that a hundred years ago the family and the neighborhood tended to provide a setting which met many of these emotional needs. Children grew up in an environment where the nature of activities was widely open to them. Most of all they were in a situation where children were economic assets, while today they tend to be liabilities. We are not inferring that parents love their children less; we are describing the characteristics of the social climate.

Adults had generally a more friendly atmosphere in which to live. There were plenty of frustrations and many communities were narrow, bigoted, and meager in the kinds of experience available. At the same time, the level of aspiration was more modest, and for most people the general acceptance by one's neighbors and the knowledge that God was in his heaven gave a serenity that seems less evident today.

3. *The changes in behavior that represent learning result from practice in activities that* the learner *finds help him achieve his goals.*

People learn what they practice only if that practice is related to *their* needs. They will learn most effectively to maintain their health when they have practice in health-maintaining activities under circumstances that make them feel that such practices help them achieve some of their own purposes. If people are to learn to behave democratically they must practice democratic behavior under circumstances that cause them to associate democratic behavior with the achievement of their own purposes. If at the same time in other situations undemocratic behavior works for them—or for others with whom they are closely associated—they will tend to become confused and frustrated.

It is desirable to help the learners appraise the consequences of their learning. This enables them to (a) see the relation between the new behavior they are learning and their progress toward their goals, and (b) modify the new behavior to make it more pertinent for their purposes. Here again the need to gauge the readiness of the learner for such appraisals and to help him acquire the skills for doing it, are challenges to the skill of the teacher.

4. *The learning activities (in which pupils engage in school) must correspond as closely as possible to the behavior that is to be needed in other situations.*

Education provides the opportunity to try something and make mistakes, to repeat a way of acting with various modifications until a satisfying way is discovered. Sometimes a community situation may be found which has enough freedom to permit such experimentation on the part of the learner; sometimes it is the function of the school to set up a situation specifically planned to provide such freedom. In either case the school has a responsibility for helping the learner get the greatest possible value from the activity. He must evaluate as well as experience.

Where the learning has been proceeding in a school situation, it will be desirable to give the learner an opportunity to try out his skills in the kind of situation for which it was designed. Short of this we can never be certain that what was learned is adequate. Learners who practice classroom reading about community problems and reporting what they have read (and who feel satisfied when they do well) are learning better how to read about community problems and report their reading in the classroom. When they have participated in an actual identification and analysis of a community problem in a way which helps them achieve their own purposes *then* they are learning how to identify and analyze community problems.

5. *In greater or lesser degree whatever is learned in one context or situation is available for use in other contexts and situations.* The extent to which the learner uses today what was learned yesterday depends upon:

   a. A "native" ability to generalize. In the degree that this factor is "native" not much can be done about it, but most persons have more of this ability than they use.
   b. The similarity between yesterday's and today's situation either in respect to their objective manifestations or methods of coping with them. One of the tasks of education is to increase the degree of relationship between the situations used for learning and the later situations which the learner will meet.
   c. Practice of these dispositions, skills and understandings which increase the range of situations to which learning can be applied. Activities such as looking for big ideas, seeking relationships, and formulating hypotheses help to improve one's ability to generalize.

STUDIES OF GROUPS

Another resource of value in meeting the larger community problems of today is the research relating to groups. It is sometimes suggested that from the standpoint of behavior there are only individuals, and that groups are to be understood only through the actions of these members. Yet groups are realities, and the study of group actions has opened up valuable insights for all phases of action.

The research in this area of group behavior draws from many streams. Basically, sociology is the study of group behavior but psychiatry, industrial research, social psychology and anthropology have contributed greatly. Today we are less conscious of the supposed disciplinary boundaries so that happily it is not always easy to designate the area from which a contribution comes. Moreno, a psychiatrist, developed a new area called sociometry; to this Lewin and his colleagues and Mayo and his colleagues have been a few of the important contributors.

1. *The group in modern society is becoming increasingly important as a unit of action.*

It perhaps would be more accurate to say that a variety of groups are becoming the units of action. The family and the town in earlier American society were the vital units. When we talk about American individualism let us recognize that the family had a great deal to do with providing strength for this individualism. The co-operative efforts of all ages—parents, children and grandparents—built a self-sufficiency which made individualism possible.

Today the family is still an important unit and it is the "family" income which enables many persons to enjoy a higher standard of living. At the same time the family has lost many of its functions and these have been taken over by various community groups. It is through these groups that the individual can make himself felt. Since these groups are not ones in which the individual grows up, he needs more help in learning the skills necessary for working in them.

2. *Group skills are complex and difficult to acquire.* In the more homogeneous life of 1850 the individual tended to get long experience in adjusting to the groups of which he was a member. In the more mobile twentieth century the diverse groups give less chance for the necessary practice and make greater requirements on each individual. We therefore become much more aware of the importance of the opportunity to learn group skills.

The more recent research has served to identify the different aspects of the group process so that definite instruction can be provided for acquiring the appropriate skills. An action group needs to clarify jobs to be done, assign responsibilities, and evaluate results. If it has persons who can cover these roles strongly it will be more effective than it would be if its members were not skilled in these activities. The work of the National Training Laboratory in Group Development, sponsored by the National Education Association and the Research Center for Group Dynamics at the University of Michigan, is significant in this connection.

3. *The heart of group activity is in the personal relationships among its members.*

Research in a factory revealed that the productivity of a group of workers was influenced greatly by the relationships among them. When one member was removed and replaced by another, the production of the group dropped markedly, although the technical skill of the new person was entirely adequate.

When two persons meet, each may feel a reaction of attraction, repulsion, or indifference. The respective reactions of each are not necessarily identical so that various combinations of attitudes are possible. Sometimes the same person will have opposite or ambivalent reactions toward another. Attitudes are modified as the persons work together. The identification of attitudes, the development of ways of getting the best possible combinations, and the modifications of attitudes are areas for which skills are being developed.

One interesting discovery in the field of groups is the part played by informal or autonomous groups. These provide certain important satisfactions for their members which center chiefly around the liking to be together. While many of these groups have definite action projects, these seem to be less important than just the fact of being with one another.

4. *A broader concept of leadership is spreading responsibility more widely throughout the community.*

One of the interesting developments of the past two decades has been an increasing understanding of the nature of leadership. The realization of the different roles which frequently have been assumed by the same person led to patterns which divided these roles among a number of different persons. While this approach is still in its infancy, it has the potentiality of drawing on a large number of persons in the community. This in turn will call for educational efforts to prepare these people for such responsibilities. The work of some volunteer officers during World War II was a good illustration of what might be done.

5. *Group situations can provide an excellent way of teaching interpersonal skills.*

Because of the importance of the emotional aspect in situations involving human relations, just talking about what should be done falls short in many cases of giving the necessary skills. If the problem is how to get a key person to agree to some action, there would be value in a discussion of various possible approaches. Still more effective is to create a situation in which persons play the roles involved. In this way aspects of the situation are often revealed which would otherwise escape notice.

6. *At the community level, there is increased study of ways of getting groups to work together.*

The experimentation on this aspect of group action is informal and there is great need for more combined efforts of social scientists and community workers. The Ogdens in

Virginia, Alinsky in Chicago, Brownell in Montana have described some of these efforts.[1] The vitality which local leadership can show is heartening.

One of the major problems is that of timing on the use of various experts. Too early use often seems to kill the local initiative. On the other hand the activity may fail for lack of technical guidance.

Another phase of this problem of intergroup action is the effort to integrate the social, religious, and ethnic groups. A number of outstanding research studies are now available in this area. The work of the American Council on Race Relations and that of the National Conference of Christians and Jews through the American Council on Education are illustrations.

STRENGTH IN THE AMERICAN WAY

In addition to the resources available in our growing insights into the nature of learning and of the group process, there should be added another of a somewhat different kind. That is the rich variety of life today. In spite of the threat of world struggle, with the inevitable channeling of a larger share of our national wealth into defense activities, we still have great resources. We have not yet learned how to use to greatest advantage the radio and television, the movies, the press and social travel, but we believe we can. We have not yet learned how to use the variety of individual and group contributions which are represented in our population and in visitors from other lands, but we can. We have not yet learned to make full use of the infinite number of

[1] See Bibliography in Chapter 8.

exciting activities going on throughout the world, but we will. The strength of democracy is in the possibility of using all these resources and creating or developing new ones. The growing realization of this tremendous potential has been one of the factors in the efforts toward a community school.

EMERGING ROLE OF THE SCHOOL

We return to our consideration of the problem of education and the role of the school. The logic of the presentation so far has been as follows:

1. The changes in our way of life over the past century or so have called for new patterns of action. This has affected the general picture of community organization as well as of education. It has meant new demands on the schools, but these generally have not been seen in relation to other developments in our culture.

2. The history of public schools during this period shows a continuous search for ways of improving the learning process. This is involved in the search both for a more potent dynamics and for techniques for acquiring attitudes, skills and knowledges when motivation is strong. The activities which we have been examining in this report under the label of Community Schools, are a part of this continuous search.

3. Parallel with these developments in education have been the developments in the community. Particularly in the past decade there has been increased stress on the importance of the local geographic unit as a vital setting for democratic processes. The feelings of frustration on the part of many individuals because the processes by which social action is

achieved seemed so unrelated to individual activities have
led to increased emphasis on the part which face-to-face
groups could play.

4. The developments in the social sciences and a broader awareness of democracy as a way of life have stressed the value
of action for vitalizing learning and the necessity of education for sound action. These ideas are pushing the schools
out into their communities and at the same time making the
communities more aware of the need for education.

We are at a stage then, when the joining of two strong
currents in American life may make this the time at which
a new pattern of education may be developed. Fundamentally, this will be a pattern of *community* education and the
analysis of the various aspects which will need to be dealt
with in a movement of such scope, goes far beyond the resources of the Committee who compiled this book.

We shall limit ourselves here to a few comments relating
to our analysis of the role of the schools in the total educational process.

The most basic task in each community is the assessment
of the over-all educational needs. These needs arise out of
the actions which the community is carrying on or pro-
posing. In the past this consideration of over-all educational
needs has been implicitly done and in the simpler, more
homogeneous community of a century ago this worked
fairly well. In our more complex society, more explicit
considerations must be given to this task.

A second phase of community education is the study of
the resources available for providing the education required and for making plans so that appropriate groups
carry out their respective responsibilities. Involved in this
is the resolution of groups that are now working in isolated
channels or at cross purposes and are therefore mis-educat-
ing the members with whom they deal.

We do not know how this task will be carried out. In general, it involves on a broader base many of the things now done in determining the work of the schools. The over-all responsibility for policy decisions belongs to the whole community, and we would expect it to operate through a democratically selected and representative board. This board would want some technical help but it would chiefly depend upon existing agencies like the schools, group work agencies, health agencies, agricultural extension. Whether this could be accomplished best by giving new responsibilities to the board of education and its administrative officer or in some other way, we do not know. The concept of a superintendent for community education has been suggested by Ernest O. Melby and others.

What Is the School?

When the term "school" is used, we generally think first of a building. What we have been trying to do in this report is to indicate approaches which might lead to a more accurate consideration of the functions of the school. We have tried to show that society operating through geographic groups which we have designated as communities, is concerned with influencing the direction which learning takes. This concern is particularly strong for the immature but it operates for all ages.

This effort to modify learning occurs in a variety of ways and is a far broader concept than the school. All of the different agencies and institutions of society have educational aspects.

Within this total framework of educational influences we find there are certain things which society feels cannot be left to the variety of agencies but must be assigned specifically to a particular agency if they are to be done well. This agency we designate as a school. We can define a "school," therefore, as that organized part of the total community effort which deals most systematically and continuously with the improvement of learning.

In order to see the special role of the school it is necessary to note some of the things which make education something more than the collection of experiences in which an individual engages in living in a society. Education emphasizes:

1. Selecting among the great variety of experiences possible, those which seem most appropriate for the needs and abilities of each learner, both as a unique individual and as a member of culture groups.
2. Paying attention to continuity of experience so that the cumulative effect of these experiences is the greatest possible.
3. Providing a setting in which learners have the freedom to experiment, to explore, to make mistakes, to take their own time, to try various ways of doing things.
4. Providing competent guidance in developing the necessary skills of learning.
5. Helping each learner to generalize his experiences so that they contribute most fully in new types of situations.
6. Building groups of learners that can raise the quality of experience many fold.
7. Providing a home base for these groups. Such a home base not only facilitates the work of a single group, but helps in furthering co-operative relations among groups.
8. Facilitating administrative arrangements which will increase the effectiveness of the learning process—special materials, records, evaluation, and the like.

Many groups perform some of these functions to varying degrees. All agencies have selective functions, most perform some guidance functions, some may provide for group activities, all furnish actual or potential settings for learning. It is clear that, educationally speaking, there can be no sharp dividing line between the school and the other agencies. The school is the agency where learning is the primary business, but so is this true of some others. It is for this reason that we have stressed the basic concept of community education.

It is important here to note that it is the community as a whole which is concerned. Legally, in American society, the "whole community" for purposes of providing schooling is the state which, in turn, with some restrictions, delegates this responsibility to the local geographic units. These local units designate certain persons to represent the community as a whole in the development of policy, and this delegated group in turn selects a professional group to execute its policies. These professional persons have the responsibility to assist the community in identifying the learning which it wants, to set priorities, and to use the most appropriate resources to achieve the educational purposes agreed upon. (It is recognized here that this is an ideal statement but we believe it is the point toward which our educational efforts with respect to the school, are directed.)

Where Is the School?

It is evident from the above that when we put the emphasis on *function* the school will be found in those activities in which persons are being deliberately assisted in learning. The school must necessarily be *of* the whole community. With this approach we can get away from the limitations which arise when we think of the school primarily in terms of a building. The school will be found in the hundreds of working relationships between groups and individuals throughout the community—twenty boys and girls planting trees under the direction of the regional forester, six children tracing the course of the local stream, a group getting information on local housing needs, two boys in the courthouse tracing the ownership of the plot on which the school stands, teen-age girls helping care for the kindergartners, an interracial committee investigating the work of human relations agencies, a subcommittee of the school board working out basic principles for a new salary schedule. Just as the agricultural extension service is not primarily located in the limited offices of the staff, but out through the entire county, so the school is where directed learning is going on.

One noticeable feature evident in many of the accounts presented is this fact that the learners are scattered throughout the community. In one of the idealized reports, it was suggested that there would be no one building corresponding to the schools as we know them. There would be a materials center and certain other centers for specific purposes. The other reports do not go this far.

The question of buildings is one on which much more study is needed. Certainly, as was suggested above, there are a number of facilities which a comprehensive educational program needs, home bases in which groups of learners can carry out certain phases of their many activities, offices for the staff, libraries, laboratories, recreation facilities, large assembly rooms, dining facilities, etc. It is likely that there will be great variation in the organization of these factors. There is value in grouping; there also is value in scattering them through the community. If the community has many resources already available among its organizations the facilities provided in the "school" might be different from those in a community with almost no such wealth of resources.

What Is the Community School?

We have completed our argument; the basic nature of the community school should now be fairly evident. Let us summarize quickly at this point.

1. "Learning" used to signify effective changes in behavior toward ends agreed upon by society, is a more limited term than "activity." Just to engage in some enterprise, even one of general social worth and one interesting to the learner, is not enough.

2. "Education" is seen as the careful planning of the activities which will foster learning and the organization of the total resources of the community for this purpose. As so defined it is a function in which the total community will participate. The fundamental value choices must be made by the whole community and the actual work with learners is done by a variety of individuals and groups. Specialists in process and in content will be needed; many of these will be part-time—giving part time to education and part time to any one of the other activities necessary in a functioning community—collecting garbage, running a church, farming, rearing a family, editing a newspaper, and so on for hundreds of other activities.

3. "Schooling" is the selection, organization and development of those educational activities which the community decides are so important that they need to be cared for by a special agency. Full use would be made of the activities of the community for educational purposes. With planning it is to be expected that many phases of living could become educational in a way similar to the educating effects of the earlier agricultural life. But we have tried to indicate that education requires the opportunity to make mistakes and sometimes when the chips are down, the stakes are too high to permit experimentation. In such cases the "school" will arrange opportunities which have a more adequate balance between vitality of incentive and demand for skills beyond the immediate level of the learner.

A "community school" may be defined, then, as that organizing of the local community efforts in such a way as to give leadership to the community's efforts to improve the learning of all its members. As was stressed above, it is seen as being *of* the whole community but it clearly has its own uniqueness. There is danger that we lose the great values of systematic instruction if we attempt to make education synonymous with life. In descending degree of comprehensiveness the order of terms is *life—learning—education—schooling*.

We have pointed out the need to distinguish between action and education. We have noted that education is a form of action, but a limited form. Education must be planned in relation to all of the actions of the community. These community actions help to determine the goals of education and they can contribute opportunities for education. But education must have a degree of freedom beyond what is ordinarily available in most community activities. As we become more skilled in education and in living, we shall expect the difference between education and general social action to lessen. Certainly education will always be one of the most important of the total activities of the community.

There are some aspects of the work of some of the community schools with which we have not directly dealt. One is the relation of the local community to larger and larger groups until eventually we reach a world organization. Another is the development of an increasingly democratic community where people have faith in one another and where opportunity for each to achieve his best is equal. Another is the development of reliance on objective consideration of facts, recognizing the part that values play but avoiding emotional bigotry. These are crucial aspects, and we believe that the approach outlined will include them. We have said that schooling takes its departure from living. We have pointed out that the functions of education are the definition of alternatives, the selection of priorities, and the development of the skills necessary to achieve the selected goals. We know that some schools which have tried to help their communities directly improve the quality of living have often been able to deal only with relatively minor problems and have sometimes abandoned co-operative efforts without ever reaching any major issues. Yet that is the calculated risk of the democratic process. As we acquire the educational skills needed to deal with the range of problems which face any community, the risk will be reduced. Recent efforts to revitalize the local community have come not as a means of escaping complex national and international problems, but rather as a way of getting groups, that could try to grapple with such larger problems, to work in a context which helped men and women see how they were related to these big questions.

It is probable that the major task at the moment is to develop administrative skill which can cope with the untidy education which results in the community approach. A group of three hundred assorted youngsters, ages five to thirteen, can be very difficult to deal with. There is something reassuring about having them in one building in a series of separate roms with definitely worked out tasks presented to them. At least there is the appearance of order.

To have these same squirming, wiggling three hundred boys and girls scattered throughout the community and sometimes scores of miles beyond, is a bit frightening. We can hear the comments: "They'll get run down"; "They'll annoy Widow Malone"; "They'll break windows"; "They'll tear their clothes"; "They certainly won't learn how to read and write."

That is the fun of the community school! It has a flavor

of the pioneer days when people moved into settings where the old answers weren't enough. Our book-focused techniques still have value as the Sloan Foundation Experiment showed, but they have to be used with many new techniques. The skills appropriate to learning how to work with others are being experimented with and as the demand rises, the scope of the experiments should rise too.

The Exciting Task

The community school is seen as a part of the larger pattern of community education in which it is the function of the school to help the whole community ("whole" being the ideal which may be progressively achieved) identify its needs, set priorities, and organize appropriate educational measures to achieve the goals sought. Many communities are still apathetic toward such a program, so the school now has the exciting task of extending its existing program in such a way as to move the community in the direction outlined.

"Community" as a functional concept means the groups and individuals who carry the action responsibilities. In actual situations this will range from towns like Visby, where power is shared by the majority of the citizens, to places where the control is pretty largely in the hands of a very small group. The school staff will need to know the situation in its community and act accordingly.

While there will therefore be variations in the approaches as has been clear in Parts I and II, we can place school activities along a rough scale in order to help schools determine their own positions. Expanding Gordon Mackenzie's scale,[2] activities might be placed somewhat as follows:

2 See *Teachers College Record*, March, 1950, pp. 347-352.

1. School tries to get community support for school program; hence information about school's program is supplied to public.
2. School uses community resources to facilitate school learning by taking children on excursions and by bringing selected contributors from community into the school.
3. Community groups use school buildings outside of school hours.
4. School studies community as it relates to subject curriculum.
5. Community uses school to facilitate civic drives such as Community Chest, March of Dimes.
6. School works to make itself an ideal democratic community.
7. School surveys, with lay advisory group, needs of community.
8. School works on service projects to improve community living.
9. School co-operates with other community agencies in some sort of community council to determine needs, make plans, take action, evaluate results, and plan again.
10. Community becomes laboratory for school in problem-solving ventures.
11. School becomes laboratory for persons who need contacts with youth—future teachers, nurses, doctors, social workers.
12. School serves otherwise unmet needs of children and adults for work and play for year-round program.
13. There is a full-scale community co-operation in curriculum planning.
14. Machinery is set up for co-operative identifying of new community problems.
15. The community concept widens as local problems are more and more related to national and world problems.

Each school should, in light of some such scale, formulate some searching questions to which it can be sensitive as it develops its own long-range program for achieving the full development of community education. The following questions suggest possibilities. For each a descriptive scale could be developed somewhat as follows:

1	3	5
Very slightly; value to a small extent	About average for localities we know	Fully, very greatly, outstanding in this respect

1. What is our community? To what extent is it a community? What can be done to make it more of a functioning community rather than just a geographical area? Do the people actually work together, show awareness of the need for common action, communicate accurately?

2. Is the community enjoying the maximum standard of living possible with available economic and human resources?

3. Do all the members of this community enjoy living in it?

4. Do young people growing up in the community desire to stay? What percentage do stay? What percentage could find a place? How can we help persons decide?

5. Do all persons living in the community feel wanted and necessary? What differences for different age levels, sexes, races, religious and ethnic groups, status classes? Are there equal opportunities for all to learn what they need when they need it under conditions (methods, places, administrative regulations, etc.) appropriate to the needs?

6. Is there a mutually co-operative relation between the community and its regions? Are local problems seen and studied in relation to state, regional, national and international developments?

7. To what extent are the major educational problems of the community defined?

8. Is the community acquainted with educational resources inside and outside its boundaries, and is it making full use of them?

9. To what extent are the school staff members recognized and used as special resource persons?

10. Is education seen as a way of helping meet the life needs of learners, with needs defined in reference to democratic values and growth potentials?

11. Is there participation by all members of the community in the development of educational policy with appropriate consideration given to special abilities and responsibilities?

12. Is emphasis given to the use of intelligence in decision-making?
13. Is there a basis for increasing community effectiveness in the next decade?
14. Is there continuous evaluation of the educational activities in terms of improvements in the quality of living for all in the community?
15. Is there exemplification by the educational group of all those qualities stressed as important in total community action?

President Carmichael of the Carnegie Foundation for the Advancement of Teaching in the forty-fifth annual report states: "At no time in the history of this country has there been so much ferment and stir about the ends and means of education. The questions have not yet been answered, but the fact that they are being asked with such persistence and by so many is the most encouraging sign of our times." In the larger sense, these questions are never answered since each society and each time must work out its own relations. But some societies and some times have a more cogent and cohesive pattern than others. It is our belief that the effort to build the community in which action rests on education, and education utilizes the combined efforts of all phases of the community, gives an opportunity for the public school beyond that ever before attained. In this setting we can help build that society of citizens of all ages, who, secure in their richness of living, can unite with other groups throughout the world in the development of an ever-expanding democracy.

8

Reference Materials

Curriculum committees, teachers, administrators, students, board members, citizens council representatives, parent-teacher leaders and others frequently request a list of "best materials" in the community school field. In an effort to meet that need, this section annotates selected books, pamphlets and motion picture films which may be helpful to those seeking to understand the community school concept and to learn more about the purposes and procedures of existing community schools.

I. BOOKS

Alinsky, Saul, *Reveille for Radicals.* (Chicago: University of Chicago Press, 1945). Dramatic account of the Back of the Yards Neighborhood Council in Chicago, emphasizing the interrelation of economic and social problems, the need for broad local organization to represent all the people in an area, and the necessity of relating local efforts with large-scale programs for social improvement.

Association for Supervision and Curriculum Development, *Organizing the Elementary School for Living and Learning* (Washington: The Association, 1947). Chapter 3, "Toward Community Planning," discusses guides for service to the community, the elementary school as a participant in community affairs, community resources for an enriched program, school-community planning, schools as centers for community living and the community co-ordinating council.

Brownell, Baker, *The Human Community, Its Philosophy and Practice for a Time of Crisis* (New York: Harper & Bros., 1950). Lucid, charming, disturbing statement of the philosophy of community living today. The problem is how men can achieve community status which will support aspirational life in the face of the disintegrative impact of technology on out-moded cultural inheritances.

Clapp, Elsie R., *The Use of Resources in Education* (New York: Harper & Bros., 1952). A case history, telling in vivid, personalized narrative, what was actually done in two rural schools in Kentucky and West Virginia, to develop the personal and community resources which children and their families use in daily living.

Colcord, Joanna C., *Your Community: Its Provision for Health, Education, Safety, and Welfare* (New York: Russell Sage Foundation, 1949). Outlines detailed suggestions for making nontechnical studies of any community.

Cook, Lloyd A. and E. F. Cook, *A Sociological Approach to Education* (New York: McGraw-Hill, 1950). Analyzes American community life as it bears upon all aspects of school practices and community relations.

Educational Policies Commission, *Education for All American Children* (Washington: National Education Association, 1948). Describes in detail the desirable program of the life-centered community school.

Educational Policies Commission, *Education for All American Youth: A Further Look* (Washington: National Education Association, 1952). Defines and illustrates needed policies for youth education in "Farmville," "American City" and "Columbia." The essential orientation is that of the community school.

Engelhardt, N. L. and N. L. Engelhardt, Jr., *Planning the Community School* (New York: American Book Co., 1940). Discusses architectural planning for the building which is designed to operate as a community center for adults as well as community school for children.

Everett, Samuel (ed.), *The Community School* (New York: Appleton-Century, 1938). Reports the philosophy of community education, the programs and principles of nine community schools in rural and urban regions, a survey of additional community activities and an analysis of the programs in terms of basic issues.

Fox, Lorene K., *The Rural Community and Its School* (New York: Kings Crown Press, 1948). Analyzes interrelationships between rural life and education, and proposes a rural school program which relates educational patterns and practices to actual life needs.

Gold, Milton J., *Working to Learn* (New York: Bureau of Publications, Teachers College, Columbia University, 1951). Reports and evaluates many work experience programs both in America and abroad. Proposes a high school curriculum centered about man's occupational activities. Examines work experience in the light of its contribution to general education.

Hamlin, Herbert M., *Citizens' Committees in the Public Schools* (Danville, Illinois: Interstate Printers and Publishers, 1952). Samples the literature of lay participation, and suggests basic procedures in organizing citizens' committees in the public schools.

Hanna, Paul, and Research Staff, *Youth Serves the Community* (New York: D. Appleton-Century, 1936). Describes several hundred varied community service projects in public safety, civic beauty, health, agricultural, and industrial improvement, civic arts, local history, surveys, and protection of resources.

Hillman, Arthur, *Community Organization and Planning* (New York: Macmillan, 1950). Reviews the philosophy, procedures and problems of local community planning.

Ivins, Wilson H. and William B. Runge, *Work Experience in High School* (New York: Ronald Press, 1950). Defines the nature and objectives of a work experience program, with step-by-step procedures for putting such a program into operation, and suggestions on how to correlate it with the existing curriculum.

King, Clarence, *Organizing for Community Action* (New York: Harper & Brothers, 1948). Summarizes successful techniques, and illustrates with many brief cases.

McCharen, William K., *Selected Community School Programs in the South* (Nashville, Tennessee: George Peabody College for Teachers, 1948). Examines the community concept in education, describes 22 specific school programs, and analyzes their organization, administration and personnel in terms of the community school idea.

National Education Association, Department of Elementary School Principals, Twenty-Fourth Yearbook: *Community Living and the Elementary School* (Washington: The Association, 1945). Presents numerous descriptions of actual practice in both rural and urban situations. The underlying philosophy is stressed, as are tested procedures in utilizing community resources in the curriculum, building community understanding of the school, meeting new community needs and adventuring in school-community co-ordination.

National Society for the Study of Education, Fifty-Second Yearbook, Part II: *The Community School* (Chicago: University of Chicago Press, 1953). Reports, analyzes, and evaluates research findings on community school philosophy, practices, progress and problems in the United States and abroad, and in local, regional, national and international terms.

Ogden, Jean and Jess, *These Things We Tried* (Charlottesville, Virginia: University of Virginia Extension Division, 1948). Describes and evaluates a five-year experiment in community development initiated and carried out by the Extension Division of the University of Virginia.

Olsen, Edward G. and others, *School and Community* (New York: Prentice-Hall, 1945, Revised Edition 1954). Presents the philosophy and procedures of community study and service, with detailed attention to the community school movement; community analysis; community experiences through resource people, field trips, school camping, surveys, work experiences, and community service; steps in organizing a community resources program; and ways of enlisting public support through community use of school facilities, lay participation and community co-ordination.

Olsen, Edward G. (editor), *School and Community Programs* (New York: Prentice-Hall, 1949). Includes over 150 concrete illustrations of successful community study and service practice in many fields from art to zoology and at all levels from kindergarten through college and adult education.

Olson, Clara M. and Norman D. Fletcher, *Learn and Live* (New York: Alfred P. Sloan Foundation, Inc., 1946). Explains the eight-year Project in Applied Economics as developed in Kentucky, Vermont and Florida. This project sought to answer the basic question: Can school instruction raise living standards in terms of better food, clothing and housing? Results are summarized visually as well as verbally.

Poston, Richard W., *Small Town Renaissance* (New York: Harper & Bros., 1950). Dramatic account of the famous Montana Study, showing how small communities improved their own quality of living through self-study groups which eventuated in creative community action in such areas as industry, art, recreation and education.

Rugg, Harold and B. Marian Brooks, *The Teacher in School and Society* (Yonkers-on-Hudson, New York: World Book Co., 1950). Chapter 10, "The School and the Community," presents three concepts: The school as a community, the community-centered school, and the education-centered community. Each is explained as a type and illustrated concretely.

Smith, B. Othanel, W. O. Stanley and J. H. Shores, *Fundamentals of Curriculum Development* (Yonkers-on-Hudson, New York: World Book Co., 1950). Chapter 22 discusses and illustrates the three community school concepts analyzed by Muntyan: the school as a model community, community activities in the school for school purposes and for community purposes, and school activities in the community for school purposes and for community purposes.

Yeager, William A., *School Community Relations* (New York: The Dryden Press, 1951). An encyclopedic treatment with chapters on such general topics as pupils, finance, and the board of education, as well as dealing with specific problems including concepts of school-community relations and the community school.

II.   PAMPHLETS

Association for Supervision and Curriculum Development, *Building Public Confidence in Our Schools* (Washington: National Education Association, 1949). Gives timely illustrations of how schools work with community groups in improvement of instructional problems.

238 EDUCATING FOR DYNAMIC DEMOCRACY

Bard, Harry, *Teachers and the Community* (New York: National Conference of Christians and Jews, 1952). Describes the Baltimore in-service program of teacher education for community understanding and participation. This program operates on a three-year cycle, and emphasizes the close interrelationship between the child, the community and the curriculum.

Blackwell, Gordon W., *Toward Community Understanding* (Washington: American Council on Education, 1943). Reports and analyzes the community study and service programs of teacher education carried on in sixteen outstanding institutions. Practical suggestions are offered.

Brown, Muriel W., *Partners in Education* (Washington: Association for Childhood Education International, 1950). Guide to better home-school relationships, with examples of co-operation in developing the curriculum, working out policies, strengthening school-community relationships, and finding and educating leaders in the community.

Hamblen, Stewart B. and Richmond Page, *Improvement of Living Through the Schools* (January 1951. Publisher not stated. 69 pp.). Describes and evaluates the American Association of Colleges for Teacher Education participation in the Project in Applied Economics of the Alfred P. Sloan Foundation.

Koopman, Margaret O., *Utilizing the Local Environment* (New York: Hinds, Hayden, and Eldredge, 1946). Outlines the philosophy and objectives of community study, with directions for making social-process local surveys, for compiling and interpreting survey findings, and for utilizing results.

Lund, S. E. Torsten, *The School-Centered Community* (New York: Anti-Defamation League, 1949). Challenges adult education to use local communities as laboratories in which to help citizens learn about race relations, labor, public services, natural resources and rural problems.

Mackintosh, Helen K., *Camping and Outdoor Experiences in the School Program* (Washington: U.S. Office of Education, 1947). Describes school camping programs of varied kinds and suggests practical ways of starting an outdoor education program.

McCharen, W. K., *Improving the Quality of Living* (Nashville, Tennessee: George Peabody College for Teachers, 1947). Presents 22 case stories of school programs in the South which are trying to serve the needs and interests of the people living in their respective communities. This pamphlet is part of the author's *Selected Community School Programs in the South.*

Metropolitan School Study Council, *Public Action for Powerful Schools* (New York: Bureau of Publications, Teachers College, Columbia University, 1949). Reports an extensive study of lay participation in school program planning. Basic principles and various patterns of public participation are discussed.

Metropolitan School Study Council, Committee on Human Resources, *Fifty Teachers to a Classroom* (New York: Macmillan, 1951). Describes plans used in various schools for finding and bringing into the classroom the talents and services of lay people as a means of enriching learning.

National League of Women Voters, *Know Your Town* (Washington: The League, 1949). Lists questions to be used in studying a town's history, government, population, industry, workers, public welfare, education, health, recreation, courts, streets, housing, etc.

Olsen, Edward G., *Social Travel: A Technique in Intercultural Education* (New York: Hinds, Hayden and Eldredge, 1947). Describes and analyzes field trip programs for children, youth and adults whereby intercultural attitudes may be improved.

Southern Regional Council, Inc., *Your Community Looks at Itself* (Atlanta: the Council, undated. 68 pp.). A manual for the home town self-survey of such factors as population, hospital facilities, recreation, law enforcement, housing and the like. Reproduces an information questionnaire for each area, and suggests basic principles and procedures to follow in making the survey.

Storen, Helen F., *Laymen Help Plan the Curriculum* (Washington: Association for Supervision and Curriculum Development, National Education Association, 1946). Analyzes forms of lay participation and offers problems and suggestions for more effective effort.

Tidwell, R. B., *Planning Improvement in Rural Living Through the Schools* (Studies in Education No. 4. University, Alabama: Bureau of Educational Research, College of Education, 1943).

Reports on exploratory study of possibilities for improving living among rural people through the agency of the public schools.

United States Office of Education, *Schools Count in Country Life* (Bulletin 1947, No. 8. Washington: Government Printing Office, 1947). Describes newer programs of education through which schools in rural communities are using their resources to improve actual living conditions.

University of Minnesota, College of Education, *Using Community Resources: Illustrative Experience Units for Grades One to Six* (Minneapolis: University of Minnesota Press, 1948). Tells how community resources enrich learnings, discusses the nature of experience units and outlines nine sample units in various interest areas.

Wisconsin Community Organization Committee, *Teamwork in the Community* (July, 1951. Publisher not stated). Brief manual presenting in question and answer form the why and how of community councils.

III. MOTION PICTURES

And So They Live. 25 min. (New York University Film Service, 1940). Presents a dramatic, documentary record of home, school and community in a section of the rural South. It shows the struggle to live in a region where the soil is depleted, where the school curriculum is far removed from the needs of the people.

Campus Frontiers. Color, 28 min. (Association Films, 1942). The work-study program at Antioch College, showing how job experience invigorates classroom study and promotes good citizenship.

Children Must Learn. 13 min. (New York University Film Service, 1940). Life of a poor family in the rural South trying to subsist on a poor soil is graphically portrayed. Suggests the part the school has played in the lives of such people and points the way to a school curriculum that deals with the problems of living.

Community Resources in Teaching. 20 min. (Iowa State University, 1950). Shows how the community and its resources, and the school and its functions, can be woven together by bringing the students into the community to use its resources as laboratory studies, and by inviting lay people into the school as speakers and demonstrators. The planning, executing, and follow-up of a class field trip are shown in detail.

Field Trip. Color, 10 min. (Virginia Department of Education and Norfolk County Schools). Shows how a junior high school biology class plans, conducts and follows up an excursion into Dismal Swamp. Objectives, preliminary reading, committee activities, student reporting, discovery of new problems and many suggestions for all types of trips are stressed.

The Lambertville Story. 20 min. (Teaching Film Custodians, 1949). The true story of a constructive community activity to establish a Saturday night teen-age recreation center. A motor accident involving adolescents shocks the citizens into a realization of their responsibility to provide wholesome recreation.

Learning Democracy Through School-Community Projects. B-W or color, 20 min. (Locke Films, 1947). Elementary and high school students participate in school councils, a rural field day, safety patrols, clean-up campaign, vocational guidance conference, Red Cross work, the parent-teacher-student organization, a community council meeting and a youth center.

Lessons in Living. 22 min. (Brandon, 1945). Shows how a school project revitalized a community by giving the children a part in community life. The community of Lantzville, British Columbia, a cross-section of nationalities and industrial groups—farmers, fishermen, lumbermen, and railroad workers—had a dispirited public school. The school and community changed and this film is the story of their transformation. The participation of children and parents in changing the school environments and in finding ways to open up recreational activities in the community is outstanding.

Living and Learning in a Rural School. 16 min. (New York University Film Service). This film shows what can be done in community education with resourceful planning. Community resources and community leadership contribute greatly to the curriculum.

Make Way for Youth. 22 min. (Association Films, 1947). The story of a mid-west community where youths of all racial backgrounds developed a youth council and recreational committee, and thus did much to reduce prejudice through community improvement.

Near Home. 25 min. (International Film Bureau, 1946). A class and teacher study the community in which they live. In the study of the community the pupils, and the part played by the teacher, can be observed in a learning process that takes advantage of an inherent interest in things near by and approaches the learning process as problem solving.

Outside School Walls. 15 min. (New Jersey State Teachers College, Montclair, 1950). Demonstrates the technique of conducting a field trip by portraying a junior high school class visit to the headquarters of the United Nations.

Playtown, U.S.A. 23 min. (Association Films, 1946). Designed to provide civic, patriotic, service, religious, social and other groups with the "why" and "how" of community organization for a year-round, all-age recreation program. This shows how a community can provide an adequate all-age recreation program if a few citizens want it.

Pop Rings the Bell. 23 min. (National School Service, 1944). A dramatized story of a typical school which is meeting the new demands on education. School taxes are shown to be an investment, not a burden.

The School and the Community. B-W or color, 14 min. (McGraw-Hill, 1952). How the school and its community can be welded into a working partnership to which each contributes and from which each draws its rightful share of mutual benefits.

School in Centerville. B-W or color, 20 min. (National Education Asociation, 1950). Shows how education in rural schools can be geared to the problems of learning to live in the community. Seventh grade classes are seen in action. Students are at work on projects which relate both to their need for knowledge and to the future roles they will take in their communities. The three R's are not neglected, but are integrated into meaningful study and activity.

School That Learned to Eat. Color, 22 min. (General Mills, 1948). Tells the story of a school that learned to eat by working and playing together. Illustrates preplanning activities of faculty and community workers; mobilization of community resources; close co-operation between home and school; classroom activities. Shows how a school-community program brought about improvement in conditions that lead to better health and nutrition.

Schoolhouse in the Red. Color, 42 min. (Agrafilms, 1948). Deals with the sociological and psychological factors involved when small communities face up to the problem of joining their school districts onto a larger unit.

School Time in Camp. Color, 18 min. (Life Camps, 1947). Two groups of children go to camp for a three-week period during the regular school terms. Boys and girls are seen retaining vivid experiences.

Tale of Two Towns. B-W or Color, 45 min. (Agrafilms, 1952). Shows how two neighboring Michigan communities co-operate to improve their community school system.

U.S. Community and Its Citizens. 20 min. (United World Films, Educational Film Dept., 1945). Portrays a community survey made by school children to study the actual functioning of community life and services. Emphasizes the fact that the community is a center of living where people depend upon each other.

Wilson Dam School. 25 min. (Tennessee Valley Authority, 1942). Shows a school designed to take care of the needs of children in the elementary school. The experiences of children, the democratic planning together of teachers and children, and the use of the community as a laboratory for learning, help point the way for the enrichment of programs in our elementary schools.

Index

APR 24 1990